AF580026

MONARCH
PRESS

TEST YOUR MARRIAGE I.Q.

TEST YOUR MARRIAGE I.Q.

by MARCIA ROSEN
in consultation with
JOANNA MAGDA POLENZ, M.D.

MONARCH PRESS
• New York •

Published by MONARCH PRESS
A Division of Simon & Schuster, Inc.
Simon & Schuster Building
1230 Avenue of the Americas
New York, New York 10020

MONARCH PRESS and colophon are registered trademarks of Simon & Schuster, Inc.
Designed by Irving Perkins Associates
Manufactured in the United States of America
10 9 8 7 6 5 4 3 2 1

Library of Congress Catalog Card Number: 83-62911

ISBN: 0-671-49973-4

The author would like to acknowledge Gerry Hunt and Northern News Service for the valuable help given in the preparation of this book.

For Herb,
with love

Contents

Introduction

Now more than ever before, marriage promises several exciting possibilities. The typical traditional family, which used to be what marriage was all about, is only one approach. Today couples are finding choices and options such as they've never known in the past.

There are blended families, reconstructed families; there are the childless or sexless or second, third and fourth marriages, as well as career couples who think nothing of commuting across country on weekends to a common home.

People want a lot out of their relationships nowadays, and they're willing to work hard to get it.

No matter what type of special arrangement you prefer, the reason for marriage remains the same as it has always been, namely to find someone with whom you can live in happiness for a lifetime.

That's where *Test Your Marriage I.Q.* can help you. Divided into three parts, each section examines a separate stage of the marital process. Whether you're just beginning to think about matrimony, or seriously considering someone in particular, or even if you've already marched down the aisle, these quizzes can increase your chances for success.

Part One consists of eleven quizzes that will help you determine if you have the personality for marriage. The more you know about your own virtues and vices, the easier it will be to judge how well you can adapt to living with someone else.

Part Two describes in ten quizzes, which add up to your own Perfect Mate Profile, how to pick the right partner, and who not to pick.

Part Three is designed for couple participation. After you and your spouse take the eighteen quizzes, you can compare your scores and answers, and then rate your chances for continued marital success.

The Conclusion, which wraps up everything you've learned so far, can act as your road map to marital happiness. There you will finally find out just what it takes to make a relationship work with the person of your choice.

Now the rest is up to you. Good luck!

Test Instructions

Test Your Marriage I.Q. is divided into three parts. It can work for you whether you're single, engaged, or already married. All you need to do is find the section that fits your current needs, get your pencil ready and answer the questions as honestly as possible.

If you find that your response would fall between some of the answer choices, select the answer which is closest to your true feelings.

Remember: Although cheating might give you a perfect score, it would be better to end up with a low score obtained honestly (which can be a useful guide to self-improvement) than to score 100 percent of what would amount to nothing.

When you are finished, you will have a composite description of your needs and wants; your special requirements in a mate; your own personal Marriage Potential Score and an overall marriage rating.

Guidelines for scoring appear at the end of each section.

Remember: These results are here to help you. So, don't get upset if your score is lower than what you had anticipated. The way you answer a question today might change a week from now after some self-inspection and insight. And you can always go back and repeat the quizzes, which could be a good way for you to record any positive growth in attitude that you might make in the future.

And if marriage is what you have in mind, this book can turn you into a perfect marriage find.

ARE YOU READY FOR MARRIAGE?

PART One

ARE YOU READY FOR MARRIAGE? While living alone can seem like a pretty grim prospect, most people will agree that living in an exclusive love relationship with another person can be just as difficult.

Like everything else in life, marriage has its ups and downs. And certain people are better able to cope than others. What are these magical characteristics that can make marriage right for you?

In the following eleven quizzes you can get a good idea of the types of personalities that fare best in lifetime commitments. After you have finished going through them, you'll understand what makes you tick, what satisfies you the most, how well you can adjust to another's needs, and what areas of your feelings and expectations, if any, need to be improved.

You'll also learn how to identify and watch out for signs that may mean you're not ready now to live in close harmony with another.

Although the conclusions you arrive at aren't absolute, they will give you a pretty accurate picture of yourself. Only after you have achieved a clear understanding of who you are and what you want out of life will you be ready to share your dreams, goals, triumphs and failures with another.

QUIZ 1

How Much Intimacy Can You Handle?

1. Do you like people who express their feelings?
   (a) yes (b) sometimes (c) no

2. Do you only like people who have a lot of information to share?
   (a) no (b) sometimes (c) yes

3. When a friend tells you about a sad event, i.e., a death in the family or the loss of a job, do you get uncomfortable and try to change the subject?
   (a) never (b) sometimes (c) always

4. Do you choose your friends because they like to do the same things you like to do?
   (a) sometimes (b) yes (c) no

5. When you go to the movies with people and they cry, do you get embarrassed and refuse to go with them again?
   (a) never (b) sometimes (c) always

6. If you're out on a first date with someone and spend most of the evening talking, do you consider this to be the most boring evening of your life?
   (a) no (b) sometimes (c) yes

7. Do you think you're having a good conversation when the other person does most of the talking?
   (a) sometimes (b) yes (c) no

8. Would you join your company's softball team because it meant a chance to meet new people?
   (a) yes (b) sometimes (c) no

9. Would you feel that it's necessary for you to reveal all the details of your past love affairs to your current love interest?
   (a) never (b) sometimes (c) always

10. On a first date, would you like to have some kind of physical contact with the other person?
    (a) yes (b) depends (c) no

11. Is it easy for you to let yourself go in front of other people?
    (a) yes (b) sometimes (c) no

12. Do you feel the man should always be the one to ask the woman out for a date?
    (a) always (b) sometimes (c) never

13. Does the unexpected, whether pleasant or unpleasant, make you feel uncomfortable?
    (a) seldom (b) never (c) always

14. Do you enjoy doing things with other people rather than alone?
    (a) yes (b) sometimes (c) no

15. Do you feel that the way people behave toward each other on a day-to-day basis is what matters most in a relationship?
    (a) yes (b) sometimes (c) no

16. Would you join your company's bowling team simply to increase your chances for a promotion?
    (a) never (b) maybe (c) always

17. Would you date somebody who didn't share your similar taste in food and cultural events?
    (a) no (b) maybe (c) yes

18. Would you feel you had to go along with your co-workers on their weekend get-togethers, just so they wouldn't talk about you?
    (a) no (b) depends (c) yes

19. If you and a date are at the amusement park for the first time and your date gets sick, would you get angry at having your evening ruined and dump him/her at the first comfort station?
    (a) never (b) probably (c) yes

20. Are you the type of person to keep secrets from close friends?
    (a) no (b) depends (c) yes

QUIZ 2

What's Your Boiling Point?

1. When your plane (train or bus) gets delayed, do you become so angry that you yell at the ticket taker?
   (a) never (b) depends (c) always

2. If your hairstylist did a bad job on your hair, would you grab the comb and try to fix it yourself?
   (a) never (b) depends (c) always

3. If you're running late for an affair and notice a spot on your outfit, would you refuse to go?
   (a) no (b) maybe (c) yes

4. If you're out with a friend who reprimands you about something you've just done, would you get angry and refuse to see that person again?
   (a) no (b) maybe (c) yes

5. If a co-worker broke a lunch date with you at the last minute, would you slam the phone down without giving the person a chance to explain and refuse to eat for the rest of the day?
   (a) never (b) maybe (c) certainly

6. If you're getting ready to give a business presentation and discover at the last minute that the slides you ordered aren't ready, would you explain what happened and give the talk anyway?
   (a) yes (b) maybe (c) no

7. If you're playing a friendly game of tennis and lose by one point, would you demand a rematch until you can get even?
   (a) no (b) maybe (c) yes

8. If a friend won a competition in which you're both entered, would you be so jealous that you couldn't congratulate the person?
   (a) no (b) maybe (c) yes

9. If you and a friend go shopping for party clothes and once there see that he/she gets more attention and compliments than you, would you get angry and hide out in a corner all evening?
   (a) no (b) maybe (c) yes

10. If you're at a picnic and your friends start up a game of touch football, which you haven't played in years, would you join the game, knowing that you will not be very good?
    (a) no (b) maybe (c) yes

11. If you just won a golf game by one point, would you be so impressed with yourself that you talk about it all day?
    (a) never (b) maybe (c) yes

12. When you're in a terrific mood, do you expect everyone else around you to feel the same way?
    (a) no (b) sometimes (c) yes

13. Do you like listening to friends talk about their good fortune?
    (a) yes (b) seldom (c) no

14. If you didn't get the promotion you wanted, would you stew about it for days afterward?
    (a) no (b) maybe (c) yes

15. If you're talking to someone when the phone rings, would you get so angry about your conversation being interrupted that you would refuse to let the person take the call?
    (a) no (b) maybe (c) yes

16. If you're at the racetrack and losing badly, would you make one last big bet hoping to change your luck?
    (a) no (b) maybe (c) yes

17. Do you find you get into moods that you hold onto for a long time?
    (a) never (b) seldom (c) always

18. Could you resist a good sale, even though it's not something you really need?
    (a) always (b) seldom (c) never

19. Do you think daydreaming is a pleasant way to pass the time?
    (a) never (b) sometimes (c) always

20. Suppose a neighbor just won a lottery. Are you likely to go out and buy ten tickets thinking the same luck will rub off on you?
    (a) no (b) maybe (c) yes

21. If your project at work has just been turned down, would your first thought be that your boss doesn't like you?
    (a) no (b) maybe (c) yes

22. When in line at the supermarket, would you get so agitated by the long wait that you would leave your groceries and walk out?
    (a) no (b) seldom (c) yes

23. If you're planning a picnic, would you consider an alternate place in case of rain?
    (a) yes (b) probably (c) no

24. Do you often start projects you don't finish?
    (a) no (b) sometimes (c) yes

25. When you're in a group, do you volunteer for several committees but quickly lose interest when the others back out?
    (a) never (b) seldom (c) always

26. Do you have a lot of hobby equipment at home, but somehow never seem to use it?
    (a) no (b) sometimes (c) yes

27. If you do something, do you want to see results very quickly?
    (a) never (b) seldom (c) always

28. Do you make an effort to balance your checkbook, no matter how much time it takes?
(a) yes (b) sometimes (c) no

29. Do all the books on your bookshelf have to be perfectly organized?
(a) no (b) haven't noticed (c) yes

30. Would you make an effort to prepare a special dinner if your boss was coming over?
(a) yes (b) depends (c) no

QUIZ 3

Do You Consider Yourself to Be a Sensitive Person?

1. Do you think teachers are always right?
(a) sometimes (b) never (c) always

2. If your company was having a party, would you decide to buy a new outfit because everybody else was doing it?
(a) never (b) probably (c) always

3. Do you show your sensitivity by always being on time?
(a) yes (b) seldom (c) never

4. Do you always answer your mail within the same week?
(a) never (b) seldom (c) always

5. If an invitation to a friend's party arrived while you were away, would you decide not to go because you didn't have time to respond properly?
(a) no (b) seldom (c) yes

6. Do you think you need to wear a suit to be properly dressed for work?
(a) no (b) sometimes (c) yes

7. Imagine there was a car accident outside your home in the middle of the night. Would you go outside dressed in your pajamas?
(a) yes (b) maybe (c) no

8. Before you buy an outfit, do you need to have a clear picture of just how you will look in it?
(a) no (b) maybe (c) yes

9. Before you go on vacation, do you have very definite expectations of what you want from it?
(a) no (b) seldom (c) yes

10. Do you only like to do the things at which you excel?
(a) no (b) sometimes (c) yes

11. If a friend told you about a very sad experience, would you try to share a similar experience with him/her?
(a) no (b) maybe (c) yes

12. If a friend couldn't keep a dinner date, would you be so upset that you'd end up skipping dinner completely?
    (a) no (b) probably (c) yes

13. If you sent out invitations to a party and your best friend didn't reply immediately, would you call and tell him/her not to come at all?
    (a) never (b) seldom (c) always

14. Do you always remember your friends and relatives with gifts for all the proper occasions?
    (a) never (b) sometimes (c) always

15. Do you always feel hurt if people don't remember you on special occasions?
    (a) no (b) seldom (c) yes

16. Do movies and stories about animals move you to tears more easily than stories about people?
    (a) no (b) seldom (c) yes

17. Do you often bring home stray animals because you feel they are more loyal than people?
    (a) no (b) seldom (c) yes

18. Do you consider punctuality one of the three greatest virtues?
    (a) no (b) sometimes (c) yes

19. Do you feel that people who share their feelings have no character?
    (a) no (b) maybe (c) yes

20. Are you always suspicious of anybody who has to borrow from you?
    (a) never (b) seldom (c) always

21. Do you take pride in knowing that no matter what, people can't read your feelings from the expressions on your face?
    (a) never (b) seldom (c) always

22. Could a co-worker become your friend in three weeks?
    (a) sometimes (b) always (c) never

23. In your personal relationships, do you find that people always disappoint you?
    (a) rarely (b) sometimes (c) often

24. Do you always start friendships with great expectations?
    (a) rarely (b) usually (c) always

25. Do you think others see you as you see yourself?
    (a) rarely (b) sometimes (c) always

26. Do you love to buy gifts for new friends?
    (a) rarely (b) usually (c) always

27. Do you feel that people take advantage of you?
    (a) no (b) sometimes (c) yes

28. When people say nice things about you, do you believe them?
(a) yes (b) sometimes (c) no

29. Do you trust your friends?
(a) mostly (b) rarely (c) never

30. If you went to a doctor and received a diagnosis for a serious problem, would you seek a second opinion?
(a) yes (b) seldom (c) no

QUIZ 4

Are You Satisfied with Yourself?

1. Do you think ambitious people make better mates?
(a) depends (b) yes (c) no

2. If you're given a chance for a job promotion, would you move to another city?
(a) maybe (b) never (c) always

3. If your mate were given a choice for a better job out of town, do you think he/she should take it?
(a) depends (b) yes (c) no

4. Would you go along with your mate?
(a) depends (b) always (c) never

5. Do you think a job promotion is more important than a relationship?
(a) never (b) sometimes (c) always

6. Would you drop a friend for telling you the truth about yourself?
(a) depends (b) no (c) yes

7. If a friend said he/she was going to school and only had time to see you occasionally, is the person trying to get rid of you?
(a) no (b) depends (c) yes

8. If your friend is going to medical school or considering a similar goal which makes it impossible to make a serious commitment, would you date others?
(a) yes (b) depends (c) no

9. In the case of question 8, would you also consider dropping the person completely?
(a) no (b) depends (c) yes

10. If you're going on a picnic, do you have to feel that you've prepared the best dish?
(a) no (b) maybe (c) yes

11. When buying your friend a gift, do you have to know that it's the most expensive one?
(a) no (b) maybe (c) yes

12. When you go to a club wearing jeans and see a sign saying proper tennis clothes required, are you hurt when you're asked to leave?
    (a) no (b) maybe (c) yes

13. At work, could you understand someone else getting a raise before you?
    (a) no (b) maybe (c) yes

14. Would you be very insulted if you lost a contest in which you thought you'd be a sure bet to be a winner?
    (a) no (b) maybe (c) yes

15. If you fell behind at work because of some uncompleted projects, would you try to blame it on a co-worker?
    (a) no (b) maybe (c) yes

16. If you're going to a party and you think that someone else there will be better dressed than you, would you still go?
    (a) yes (b) depends (c) no

17. Do you feel lucky when people like you?
    (a) no (b) sometimes (c) yes

18. If guests came over unexpectedly and the house was dirty, would you blame the mess on your roommate?
    (a) no (b) maybe (c) yes

19. As a child, were your parents very understanding of you?
    (a) depends (b) usually (c) always

20. Do you fear that if people knew the real you, they wouldn't like you very much?
    (a) no (b) sometimes (c) yes

21. Do you feel good about yourself most of the time?
    (a) yes (b) depends (c) no

22. When you feel lonely and go see a friend, do you expect them to drop everything and do what you want to do?
    (a) never (b) sometimes (c) always

23. Do you think your parents were fair with you when you were a child?
    (a) yes (b) sometimes (c) no

24. Whenever you undertake a project, is your first question "What's in it for me?"
    (a) no (b) depends (c) yes

25. Do you think it's important to have the best clothes or the best car to impress your friends?
    (a) no (b) yes (c) maybe

26. Do you always arrange your work time so you'll have part of the day left to exercise?
    (a) yes (b) depends (c) no

27. Do you faithfully set aside some time each week to take care of your grooming needs?
    (a) always (b) depends (c) not usually

28. Would you take a second job to pay off your membership at a health club?
    (a) yes (b) maybe (c) no

29. If a best friend kept insisting that he/she's got the perfect date for you, would your first question be, "What does the person look like?"
    (a) no (b) depends (c) yes

30. Do you like to look neat and clean, even when lounging around the house?
    (a) yes (b) depends (c) no

31. Is your closet so disorganized that most of the time you'll just grab the first outfit you can lay your hands on?
    (a) no (b) depends (c) yes

32. Do clothes and grooming products take the most money out of your budget?
    (a) yes (b) depends (c) no

33. Do you feel uncomfortable when other people look at you?
    (a) no (b) depends (c) yes

34. When going to a party, would you hate to make an entrance alone?
    (a) no (b) depends (c) yes

35. Are you always careful about what you eat and drink?
    (a) usually (b) yes (c) no

QUIZ 5

Can You Cooperate with Others?

1. If your current date's job kept him/her tied up three weekends out of four, and you didn't like this arrangement, would you ask if something could be done about it?
   (a) yes (b) depends (c) no

2. If your roommate just ran out of deodorant, would you tell him/her to go out and buy some and refuse to lend yours?
   (a) no (b) depends (c) yes

3. If it's your roommate's turn to do the grocery shopping and he/she has to work overtime, would you do it as a favor?
   (a) yes (b) depends (c) no

4. If you're in a big hurry and spot your neighbor struggling with some packages, would you help knowing that it will make you late?
   (a) yes (b) depends (c) no

5. If you have nothing else to do at work, would you offer to help others?
   (a) yes (b) depends (c) no

6. If your roommate wants to borrow your car, and there's a slight chance you might want to use it yourself, would you still lend it to him/her?
   (a) yes (b) depends (c) no

7. If your roommate begs off of walking the dog every time it rains, would you do it but make a point of saying it's unfair?
   (a) yes (b) depends (c) no

8. Is it fair to let your friend use his/her car and gas most of the time, when you both go out on trips together?
   (a) no (b) depends (c) yes

9. If you're working on a committee, should you always try to be the chairperson?
   (a) no (b) depends (c) yes

10. If you're given some assignments to do at work, which you're supposed to share with other co-workers, do you try to select the easiest ones for yourself?
   (a) no (b) depends (c) yes

11. Is singling out the best assignments for yourself a smart thing to do?
   (a) no (b) depends (c) yes

12. If you only have enough money to buy one candy bar, would you wait until you're alone and eat it yourself?
   (a) no (b) depends (c) yes

13. If you're sharing a bedroom and want the space by the window, would you reciprocate and give your roommate the larger dresser?
   (a) yes (b) depends (c) no

14. If you and a co-worker are given the job of getting out your company's annual report, would you make sure the other person did most of the work, even though you're both going to be taking equal credit?
   (a) no (b) depends (c) yes

15. If you're taking a shower and realize there isn't much hot water left, would you cut down your time so your roommate could also take one?
   (a) yes (b) depends (c) no

QUIZ 6

How Competitive Are You?

1. Do you like to take risks just for the thrill of it?
   (a) yes (b) depends (c) no

2. Do you even enjoy a good scare once in a while?
   (a) yes (b) depends (c) no

3. Do you go out of your way to find dangerous situations?
   (a) yes (b) depends (c) no

4. Do you like to participate in group sports?
   (a) yes (b) depends (c) no

5. Do you find the more you have to fight for something, the less you want it?
   (a) no (b) depends (c) yes

6. Do you find your fears often prevent you from doing what you'd like to do?
   (a) no (b) depends (c) yes

7. Are you the type that acts first and asks questions later?
   (a) yes (b) depends (c) no

8. Would you ever show up at work in a pair of jogging shorts?
   (a) yes (b) depends (c) no

9. Would you be more interested in a date if he/she played hard to get?
   (a) yes (b) depends (c) no

10. Would something seem more valuable to you if you had to go to extraordinary lengths to own it?
    (a) yes (b) depends (c) no

11. Do you prefer taking vacations that are sports-oriented rather than just lying on a beach?
    (a) yes (b) depends (c) no

12. Would you do almost anything to win?
    (a) yes (b) depends (c) no

13. If you were turned down for a raise and you thought the reasoning was unfair, would you fight for your rights?
    (a) yes (b) depends (c) no

14. Would you fear the insecurity of being self-employed?
    (a) no (b) depends (c) yes

15. Do you believe in living for today because tomorrow will take care of itself?
    (a) yes (b) sometimes (c) no

16. Do you often wish you could have lived in the Old West when men were men and women were women?
    (a) yes (b) depends (c) no

17. Do you get bored with someone who is not as action-oriented as you are?
    (a) yes (b) sometimes (c) no

18. Do you like to follow a very predictable schedule in your life?
    (a) no (b) depends (c) yes

19. Do you like to play games which are a test of skill?
    (a) no (b) depends (c) yes

20. Do you have strong goals mapped out for your future?
    (a) yes (b) in some cases (c) no

QUIZ 7

Can You Communicate with Others?

1. If your roommate liked one candidate and you another, would you refuse to get into a political discussion because you didn't want to hear the other person's point of view?
   (a) never (b) sometimes (c) always

2. If your friend started to tell you about a recent vacation, would you cut the person off in order to talk about yours instead?
   (a) never (b) sometimes (c) always

3. If a friend just recommended a new restaurant, would you thank the person and write down the phone number?
   (a) always (b) sometimes (c) never

4. Do you and your roommate like to talk things over?
   (a) always (b) sometimes (c) never

5. At parties do you think the conversation men have is far more interesting than the conversation women have?
   (a) depends (b) always (c) never

6. Would you tell a lie to get ahead?
   (a) never (b) maybe (c) always

7. Would you tell a lie to protect somebody else?
   (a) no (b) seldom (c) yes

8. Do you feel more comfortable when someone else does the talking?
   (a) sometimes (b) never (c) always

9. Do you hold back a lot of your feelings simply because you hate to argue?
   (a) never (b) sometimes (c) always

10. Do you feel that when married the most important thing is to be able to communicate with your spouse?
    (a) always (b) sometimes (c) never

11. If you're having an argument and the other person starts to cry, should you give them a box of tissues and keep talking?
    (a) yes (b) don't know (c) no

12. If a person is yelling at you, should you keep talking and not let this intimidate you?
    (a) yes (b) don't know (c) no

13. If they storm out of the room, should you follow them?
    (a) probably (b) don't know (c) never

14. If they start sulking, should you stop talking?
    (a) no (b) don't know (c) yes

15. If they give you the silent treatment, should you stop talking also?
    (a) no (b) don't know (c) yes

16. Do you think a person open to suggestion is easier to communicate with?
    (a) yes (b) don't know (c) no

17. If you're very well educated, do you think your opinion should override someone who isn't?
    (a) no (b) don't know (c) yes

18. If a person is not well educated and has strong opinions, do you consider him/her stubborn?
    (a) no (b) don't know (c) yes

19. Do you think a perfectionist is easy to get along with?
    (a) no (b) don't know (c) yes

20. Do you feel most of the time people simply don't understand you?
    (a) no (b) don't know (c) yes

21. Do you think it's important to be a good listener?
    (a) yes (b) sometimes (c) no

22. Do you have trouble accepting other people's points of view, if they are different from your own?
    (a) no (b) sometimes (c) yes

23. Do you try to avoid arguments as much as possible?
    (a) no (b) sometimes (c) yes

24. Do you think you should always speak your mind?
    (a) mostly (b) sometimes (c) no

25. If there's something really important to you, do you stand fast, no matter how hard somebody tries to change your mind?
    (a) yes (b) sometimes (c) no

26. Do you think there are times when it's best to leave things unsaid?
    (a) yes (b) sometimes (c) no

27. Do you think being able to communicate with co-workers is a good sign that you'll be able to communicate with your spouse?
    (a) yes (b) don't know (c) no

28. Do you think the communication skills you will need in a marriage are completely different from the ones you would use with your friends?
    (a) no (b) don't know (c) yes

29. Do you think in answering the last five questions your judgment was good?
    (a) yes (b) don't know (c) no

30. Would you be willing to improve your judgment on these?
    (a) yes (b) don't know (c) no

QUIZ 8

Are You Willing to Please Others?

1. If your roommate made less money than you, would this make you feel superior?
   (a) no (b) don't know (c) yes

2. Do you always expect something in return for the nice things you do for other people?
   (a) no (b) usually (c) yes

3. Do you feel being near someone during a crisis is better than any money or gifts you could give them?
   (a) yes (b) don't know (c) no

4. Are you generous to praise other's accomplishments?
   (a) yes (b) seldom (c) no

5. Would you hesitate to sacrifice an important goal if it meant that a close personal friend would suffer?
   (a) no (b) usually (c) yes

6. Do you take an interest in your friends' hobbies or work only when they're similar to your own?
   (a) no (b) usually (c) yes

7. Do you always cope with your problems in the most inoffensive way possible because you don't like hurting other people's feelings?
   (a) yes (b) seldom (c) no

8. Are you willing to make a special effort to be with friends you care for?
   (a) yes (b) usually (c) no

9. Would you socialize with your roommate's friends as a favor if you didn't particularly like them?
   (a) always (b) seldom (c) never

10. When you're out with your co-workers, do you generally go along with what the group wants to do?
    (a) always (b) seldom (c) never

11. Is it easy for you to share secrets with your friends?
    (a) yes (b) seldom (c) no

12. Do you think companionship is an important reason for getting married?
    (a) yes (b) don't know (c) no

13. Are you willing to put the comfort and satisfaction of other people above your own?
    (a) yes (b) don't know (c) no

14. Do you feel it's equally important to care for someone as it is to be cared for?
    (a) yes (b) don't know (c) no

15. Is one of your reasons for getting married to do what is expected of you?
    (a) no (b) maybe (c) yes

QUIZ 9

How Well Can You Cope with Change?

1. If your relatives were coming to stay for a few days, would it make you uptight to give up your bedroom and sleep on the couch?
   (a) no (b) depends (c) yes

2. You've been driving the same route to work for years. One day you have to detour around an accident. Would this change upset your whole day?
   (a) no (b) maybe (c) yes

3. Your department is being moved to larger, more spacious quarters in another part of the building. Would you look forward to this change?
   (a) yes (b) don't know (c) no

4. Do you like to use the same cup every day for your morning coffee?
   (a) no (b) depends (c) yes

5. If someone at work took your favorite chair and didn't return it, would you feel you couldn't work as well?
   (a) no (b) maybe (c) yes

6. Every Friday night you go bowling with your friends. Would you refuse to change your schedule if something else came up?
   (a) no (b) depends (c) yes

7. For as long as you can remember, you've always parted your hair on the left side. Would you change it if your hairstylist recommended doing so?
   (a) yes (b) maybe (c) no

8. Would you turn down the chance to move to a better apartment because you couldn't bear leaving the neighborhood where you've lived for the past ten years?
   (a) no (b) depends (c) yes

9. Would you refuse to eat a hamburger with ketchup because your favorite dressing is mayonnaise?
   (a) no (b) usually (c) yes

10. If your date for the evening showed up in a bright green outfit, a color you hate, would you ask that person to go home and change?
    (a) no (b) maybe (c) yes

11. If your friend tells you about a terrific person he/she wants you to meet, would you turn him/her down if you find out the person is from another culture?
    (a) no (b) depends (c) yes

12. Every Sunday you look forward to reading the papers while eating breakfast. Would you be upset about an impending newspaper strike?
    (a) no (b) probably (c) yes

13. If a new restaurant opened in town and your roommate was dying to go, would you give it a try, even if you didn't particularly like the type of food?
    (a) yes (b) maybe (c) no

14. If you just changed your hair color, would you have to keep asking your friends if it looked good to reassure yourself that it did?
(a) no (b) maybe (c) yes

15. If a friend returns from vacation with a pretty scarf for you, would you try to wear it even if the colors were too bright for your taste?
(a) depends (b) yes (c) no

QUIZ 10

What's Your Loyalty Quotient?

1. If you wanted to go to your company's office party and your boyfriend/girlfriend didn't, would you go alone?
(a) no (b) depends (c) yes

2. Do you feel it's essential to talk over all major decisions in marriage?
(a) yes (b) depends (c) no

3. If you were married and your spouse objected to certain friends, would you stop seeing them?
(a) depends (b) yes (c) no

4. Once married, would you be willing to give up your independence?
(a) yes (b) depends (c) no

5. Would it bother you to have a public argument with a friend?
(a) no (b) seldom (c) yes

6. Would you be willing to give up some of the control you now have over your life to be with another person?
(a) yes (b) depends (c) no

7. Would you ever lie to a friend?
(a) no (b) maybe (c) yes

8. Do you feel there are degrees of being frank?
(a) no (b) sometimes (c) yes

9. Would it bother you if someone you liked was being taken advantage of?
(a) yes (b) don't know (c) no

10. When you see a friend is upset, would you try to console and offer help to the person?
(a) yes (b) usually (c) no

11. Do you find going your own way works the best for you?
(a) no (b) usually (c) yes

12. Would you rather be involved in doing something interesting with a friend than doing it alone?
(a) yes (b) depends (c) no

13. In the past, have your relationships with the opposite sex been generally good and long lasting?
(a) yes (b) seldom (c) no

14. Would you prefer having only a few friendships as long as they were dependable and long lasting?
    (a) yes (b) usually (c) no

15. If contemplating marriage or living with someone, do you think the new arrangement would be good for your personal development?
    (a) yes (b) maybe (c) no

16. Does having a close relationship with friends make you feel more confident about yourself?
    (a) yes (b) usually (c) no

17. Do you often wish you were married or living with someone?
    (a) yes (b) often (c) no

18. After knowing someone for a long time, do you find they fail to live up to your expectations?
    (a) no (b) often (c) yes

19. Which would you rate the most important out of the following items?
    (a) a close personal friendship
    (b) achievement of a personal goal
    (c) independence

20. If for some reason a friend let you down, would you forgive the person once you got over your disappointment?
    (a) yes (b) depends (c) no

QUIZ 11

Are You a Mature Person?

1. Suppose you've just missed your plane. Would you re-book on the next flight, and then find the nearest cocktail lounge and get a drink?
   (a) depends (b) always (c) never

2. Suppose you've just met someone at an airport whom you find interesting. Would you deliberately miss your plane to try to get to know the person better?
   (a) depends (b) never (c) always

3. A very good friend tells you something embarrassing about yourself. Should you say something nasty in return?
   (a) no (b) maybe (c) yes

4. You didn't get that job you wanted. Would you rush into the boss's office and tell him you quit?
   (a) no (b) depends (c) yes

5. Would you try to evaluate the competition to see why you were passed over, and then confront the boss about it?
   (a) yes (b) usually (c) no

6. If you're playing a friendly game of tennis and you feel the point is in doubt, would you ask to take it over?
   (a) yes (b) usually (c) no

7. If you want to buy a pair of shoes but can't seem to get the attention of the clerk, should you take a nearby sample shoe and bang it on the counter?
   (a) no (b) maybe (c) yes

8. Do your moods change according to the circumstances?
   (a) yes (b) usually (c) no

9. Do you use caution in all your business dealings and never go for broke?
   (a) depends (b) yes (c) no

10. Would you buy something on sale, just for the bargain, even if you didn't really need it?
    (a) no (b) sometimes (c) yes

11. If you've been planning a special trip for a long time, and at the last minute your roommate gets sick and can't go along, would you blame the person for ruining your vacation?
    (a) no (b) depends (c) yes

12. Would you alter your plans and go alone?
    (a) depends (b) yes (c) no

13. Would you try to show your roommate how sloppy he/she is by only cleaning your side of the room?
    (a) no (b) depends (c) yes

14. Do you have a fairly good sense of humor?
    (a) yes (b) usually (c) no

15. If you're about to give a talk in front of a group and you notice that your zipper's come undone, would you get so unglued that you can't continue?
    (a) no (b) depends (c) yes

Scoring Instructions for Part One

Rating

The eleven quizzes in Part One are designed to do the following:

1) Rate you on your key personality traits.
2) Show you why you would or wouldn't make a good candidate for marriage by pointing out exactly where your strengths and weaknesses lie.
3) Give you an overall Marriage Potential Score. (See page 24.)

Scoring

To convert the answers to your questions into a point value, use the following scoring system:

1) For each (a) answer—give yourself 3 points.
2) For each (b) answer—give yourself 2 points.
3) For each (c) answer—give yourself 1 point.

Add up the total number of points for each quiz separately, so that in the end, you have eleven different scores which will be important for arriving at your evaluations.

Note: use this same scoring system for all eleven quizzes.

Evaluating

Now that you've done all the hard work, you're ready to find out just where you stand in the marriage stakes. Beginning with Quiz 1, simply find the range which fits your score and read the corresponding explanation.

QUIZ 1
How Much Intimacy Can You Handle?

Intimacy is used here to mean the ability to have a close personal relationship with someone in many ways, not only sexually.

If you scored between:

50–60 You have a high capacity for intimacy. And you are not afraid to reveal yourself as you really are. For you, being in love is both a natural and pleasurable state, without any fear of rejection or loss of independence. And marriage is definitely the right course for you.

36–49 It's a little difficult for you to be intimate, although you do look forward to sharing your life with someone. But if you begin now to build more confidence in yourself, you'll be able to look forward to marriage, if only with a slight tinge of fear.

20–35 Although you may want an intimate relationship in your life, you're also frightened by the thought of it. And this means more work on your part: learning how to relate to others before taking the big step into a marital commitment.

QUIZ 2
What's Your Boiling Point?

In marriage an ideal partner needs the patience and understanding to know that every life situation doesn't bring immediate gratification.

If you scored between:

76–90 You have a high tolerance for frustration, which makes you an excellent marriage candidate.

51–75 You are still fairly flexible when it comes to understanding that you will not get what you want at all times and in all situations.

30–50 You're not really ready for marriage because you don't have the endurance to deal with a situation that isn't going to live up to your standards.

QUIZ 3
Do You Consider Yourself to Be a Sensitive Person?

In this quiz, sensitivity is being used to illustrate a lopsided overreaction on the part of one person to another's behavior.

If you scored between:

76–90 You are very secure and understand yourself, your priorities and your interests. You have no trouble trusting people and don't feel you're being taken advantage of. As a mate, you would rate an A #1.

51–75 You're not overly sensitive, but you're not totally trusting of people either. And you may want to lighten up your expectations when it comes to your own behavior and that of other people.

30–50 You're overly sensitive, and always testing people's feelings toward you, from the most intimate to the most trivial. That's because you always feel you're being taken advantage of. It's difficult for others to live up to your expectations because you set little traps guaranteeing that sooner or later they will fail. As a marriage partner, you would be very difficult to live with, unless you come to terms with your oversensitivity.

QUIZ 4
Are You Satisfied with Yourself?

How you feel about yourself affects the way you relate to others.

If you scored between:

83–105 You have a very healthy view of how and where you fit into the world, and you're capable of sharing life with another. You don't always need to have your own way, and you don't expect your every wish to be granted.

59–82 You'd be a good bet as a marriage partner as long as you learned to control your need to be indulged.

35–58 You think the world revolves around you. And, as a result, you'd find it very hard to share space in your universe with anyone else.

QUIZ 5
Can You Cooperate with Others?

Cooperation is one of the main building blocks of marriage. Without it, you would have a great deal of trouble maintaining a healthy relationship.

If you scored between:

35–45 You're a truly cooperative person. You understand that life is a series of trade-offs, where you have to please others as well as yourself. In marriage, this trait would make you a top candidate.

25–34 You're going to have to loosen up a little, and give in more often if you want to make a good spouse to someone in the future.

15–24 Marriage has to be a cooperative effort, but you're not a cooperative person. Unless you feel you want to change, you'd better think about staying single and be grateful for the sexual revolution.

QUIZ 6
How Competitive Are You?

While competitiveness is neither a negative nor a positive trait for marriage, it's good to know how you rate when looking for your ideal mate.

If you scored between:

50–60 You rank at the top of those people who enjoy the spirit of competition. Your drive is so strong, you couldn't be happy with someone who didn't share your energy and zest for challenge.

36–49 You're pretty middle-of-the-road as far as going out and fighting for what you want. Some things can really get your motor running, but you could probably relate to a high-competition as well as a low-competition personality without too many problems.

20–35 You don't like competition. As a matter of fact, you get very uncomfortable with anything except that which is status quo. You prefer the comfort of routines to risk taking. And you definitely would have problems with a mate who would rather fight than switch.

QUIZ 7
Can You Communicate with Others?

Communication is essential in a marriage; the key to a satisfactory relationship is the ability to share your thoughts, needs, goals and aspirations.

If you scored between:
76–90 You have no trouble sharing your feelings with others. As a matter of fact, you're probably quite popular, since communication is a social skill. You would also rate equally high marks as a potential marriage mate, because you are open, direct and can express yourself while listening to another's point of view.
51–75 You're willing to share some of your feelings, but most of the time you put on the brakes before letting go completely. In marriage, this could create problems, because your mate would have to be a mind reader to figure out what you're thinking.
30–50 You should really try to open up a little more. Still waters run deep, but nothing ruins a relationship faster than a partner who can't speak up about what's on his/her mind. If you're planning on living your life with someone, you have to learn how to share your thoughts, dreams, feelings and even your failures a lot more easily than you are now willing to do.

QUIZ 8
Are You Willing to Please Others?

Marriage is a partnership in which you have to make all your future decisions in relation to pleasing yourself as well as your spouse.

If you scored between:
35–45 You have no trouble understanding what it takes to make someone happy. You're quick to appreciate another's talents, and generous with praise and encouragement.
25–34 While you won't go out of your way to please someone, you're aware of how to show a person you care.
15–24 You seem to be confused about selflessness and selfishness. If you're planning to spend your life with a mate, you have to learn that it's as important to please others as it is to please yourself.

QUIZ 9
How Well Can You Cope with Change?

In marriage your life keeps changing, i.e., the introduction of children, increased intimacy, in-law interference, etc. A good marriage partner needs to be flexible enough to cope.

If you scored between:
35–45 You're a very adaptable person. This is a very important quality to bring to a marriage, because conflict and change are usually the rules rather than the exceptions.
25–34 You are uncomfortable with too many changes happening in your life, but you can still cope.
15–24 You are rigid and inflexible when it comes to change. Even the slightest deviation of schedule upsets you. And if you're thinking of marriage, you have to learn how to become much more adaptable than you are now.

QUIZ 10
What's Your Loyalty Quotient?

Loyalty is a vital marriage quality; it is the bond that will get you through the good and bad times, which are inevitable in any marriage.

If you scored between:
50–60 You have a great capacity for loyalty and commitment to another

person. And you would not let anything get in the way of your marriage.

36–49 You need to make a more conscious effort toward commitment to another person in a lifetime arrangement such as marriage.

20–35 You're not ready to give yourself entirely to one person, or value a life situation that has longevity. Since marriage demands such a life-style, it would seem that right now, at least, it's not the best idea for you.

QUIZ 11
Are You a Mature Person?

No marriage can be ideal. Although many try to fantasize it into perfection, only a mature person accepts it for its reality.

If you scored between:

35–45 You realize that no one person or situation can fulfill all your dreams, nor are you in search of any magic formulas to make your future brighter. You have a good grasp of who you are. Therefore, you'd be sure to make any marriage partner happy.

25–34 You're a dreamer, and you'd like to believe that someone else can bring you total happiness. But deep down, you know the truth, which keeps your feet on the ground after all.

15–24 You react to life's problems by hiding in dreams and fantasies, hoping to make the "gremlins" go away. And just as unrealistically, you expect marriage to be that kind of safe haven. Unfortunately no marriage can work that kind of magic.

Finding Your Marriage Potential Score (MPS)

Here's the score you've been waiting for. To find your MPS, go back to the original eleven score values and total them for what will be your MPS guide in the following ratings.

If you scored between:

574–735 You're terrific. And you shouldn't have any trouble making your marriage work. You're open, loving and giving. And even in this day and age of looking out for number one, you know the important ingredients that go into making a successful relationship.

You recognize the needs of others, respect their feelings, appreciate their differences and can readily put yourself in another person's shoes. You're willing to work at a commitment no matter what gets in the way. And you'll give 100 percent of yourself to make it grow every day.

409–573 Marriage will work well for you if you're willing to bend a little. That means learning to let yourself go a bit more and criticizing others a lot less. You also have to become less exacting of others, particularly in what you expect from your spouse; nothing in life, including marriage, is either all black or all white.

You tend to appreciate what others want and need, and respect their feelings as long as it suits you. And this is fine, providing you pick a partner who's in agreement with your points of view. That's why it's particularly important for you to be aware of your good points as well as your shortcomings; in that way you can select a mate who would compliment your personality traits in both weak and strong areas.

245–408 It's very hard to give to a relationship if there's not much to contribute in the first place. But even if you don't have the ingredients to make a perfect marriage now, anything's possible if you have the willingness to grow and change.

And the recipe is here for you to accomplish just that. All you need to do is go back and reexamine the areas where you might need improvement.

If you're not satisfied with the way you're handling certain situations in your life, or feel that you could benefit from professional help to work on some undesirable character traits, you can achieve that if you remain open and accepting of change.

Just remember that nothing happens overnight. And now's the time to build. It might take you weeks, months or even years to get to the place you'd like to be. But if you like yourself enough to make the effort, it's worth the try.

HOW TO CHOOSE A PARTNER

PART TWO

YOU'LL NEVER MAKE A MORE IMPORTANT DECISION THAN THAT OF PICKING A PERMANENT PARTNER. Some people have made up their minds about their "dream mates" in childhood. But very often, the gap between the illusion of the person you want and the reality of the one you need results in less than wedded bliss. And many a bride and groom go straight from the altar into a state of disppointment, because they married for all the wrong reasons.

Fortunately there is a formula that you can follow for finding long-lasting love. After all, who'd want to risk a lifetime of happiness on something as fickle as marriage. And this section can help you learn what that means.

Ingredient #1: Before you marry, test him/her. Granted no one knows why Mr. or Mrs. Right can push our passion buttons when other equally good prospects are left waiting in the wings.

Although opposites do attract, marital experts have found that it's not the differences, but the similarities in background, culture, education, intelligence, religion, career goals, etc., that keep two people together.

To recognize your ideal mate, you first have to understand how much you both have in common.

And that's where Quizzes 12, 13 and 14 can help. They're not to be scored. They require honesty to get at the true personalities of you and your potential partner.

After you've studied your likes and dislikes, the next seven quizzes can help you clarify your expectations on key marriage issues; that way you can select a person who will be compatible with your needs.

And that brings us to Ingredient #2. Before you marry, test yourself. You can still fantasize about your Cinderella or Prince Charming. However, based on your answers to the quiz questions, you may want to think twice about how a particular person will fit into your life's plans.

Of course, no one's going to satisfy your needs 100 percent of the time. But your test results should help you to weed out some people before deciding on the one person with whom you'd like to spend the rest of your life.

QUIZ 12

How Will You Know Your Perfect Mate?

If you already have a special someone in mind, take this quiz to determine how successful a marriage you can expect based on the number of similarities the two of you have in common.

If you simply want to know who might be best for you, you can still use this checklist to develop a personality profile of your background, tastes, interests and expectations that can be used to identify similar qualities in a suitable mate.

THE MARRIAGE CHECKLIST I

1. Do you know everything about his/her background?
2. Does he/she know everything about yours?
3. Have you met his/her relatives?
4. Has he/she met yours?

5. Does he/she know your weak points?
6. Has this person told you about his/hers?
7. Does this person have any personal problems, i.e. alcohol, drugs?
8. Do you have any personal problems that you should reveal?
9. Does this person have any serious health problems?
10. Do any of his/her family members have serious health problems, i.e., heart trouble, cancer, mental retardation, etc.?
11. Do you have a family background of health problems?
12. Are this person's parents happily married?
13. Are your parents happily married?
14. Are his/her parents divorced?
15. Are your parents divorced?
16. Is he/she in good health?
17. Are you in good health?
18. Does he/she have trouble communicating personal feelings?
19. Are you able to express your feelings to this person?
20. Do you find you keep a lot of things inside?
21. Do you think he/she tells you everything?
22. What are his/her political beliefs?
23. What are your political beliefs?
24. What are his/her religious beliefs?
25. What are your religious beliefs?
26. Did the person have a close family relationship while growing up?
27. Were you close to your parents while growing up?
28. Are you both from large families?
29. Are you both from small families?
30. How would you rate your potential mate on the following character traits? (Remember to rate yourself as well)

---

independent	( ) very	( ) not very	( ) don't know
open	( ) very	( ) not very	( ) don't know
passive	( ) very	( ) not very	( ) don't know
helpful	( ) very	( ) not very	( ) don't know
kind	( ) very	( ) not very	( ) don't know
giving	( ) very	( ) not very	( ) don't know
reassuring	( ) very	( ) not very	( ) don't know
competitive	( ) very	( ) not very	( ) don't know
cold	( ) very	( ) not very	( ) don't know
self-confident	( ) very	( ) not very	( ) don't know
able to deal with stress	( ) very	( ) not very	( ) don't know
can't cope with stress	( ) very	( ) not very	( ) don't know
a go-getter	( ) very	( ) not very	( ) don't know
energetic	( ) very	( ) not very	( ) don't know
a self-starter	( ) very	( ) not very	( ) don't know
quick to anger	( ) very	( ) not very	( ) don't know

never loses temper	( ) very	( ) not very	( ) don't know
honest	( ) very	( ) not very	( ) don't know
dependable	( ) very	( ) not very	( ) don't know
a good conversationalist	( ) very	( ) not very	( ) don't know

---

31. Are your educational backgrounds similar?
32. Are your career goals similar?
33. Do you have to make most of the accommodations to this person's needs?
34. Would he/she like to have a family?
35. Do you feel that a wife should work outside the home?
36. Does he/she agree on this?
37. Once married, who would be in charge of the finances?
38. Are you both comfortable living in the same type of climate?
39. Do you share the same hobbies?
40. Do you both have the same sports interests?
41. Are your cultural tastes similar?
42. Would you both like to live in the suburbs?
43. Would you both like to live in a big city?
44. Would his/her career create a conflict with your field of interest?
45. How far away do his/her parents live?
46. How far away do your parents live?
47. What would you say is your intended's best quality?
48. What is your best quality?
49. Do you have any physical handicaps?
50. Does he/she have any physical handicaps?
51. Are you both of the same race?
52. At this present time, are you earning more money than your potential mate?
53. Are you earning less?
54. Do you expect his/her income level to change in the next five years?
55. Are you both in similar professions?
56. Are you both in competing professions?
57. Would you both like to work together at some point in the future?
58. Do you think that the male should be the breadwinner of the family?
59. Do you feel the wife's duty is to stay home and care for the children?
60. If now working, would you maintain the job after marriage?
61. Do you like spending a lot of time alone by yourself?
62. Does your partner like being involved in lots of groups and social activities?
63. Do you intend to further your education?
64. Does the person intend to further his/her education?
65. Is your intended spouse a sensual person?
66. Is touch an important part of your lovemaking?
67. Is atmosphere an important part of your lovemaking?
68. Are you both attracted to certain perfumes?
69. Are you both attracted to the same colors?
70. Do you like to look at erotic books, photos or movies?
71. Have you ever done this together?

72. Did you have a part-time job while going to high school or college?
73. Did he/she ever work for extra money during high school or college?
74. Would you be willing to make adjustments in your life to further your spouse's career?
75. Would he/she be willing to do the same for you?
76. Are you from an affluent family?
77. Is he/she from an affluent family?
78. Do you like animals?
79. Does he/she like animals?
80. Does he/she have any personal habits or quirks that bother you?
81. Do you think you have any personal habits that would be bothersome?
82. Do you both enjoy doing the same things when on vacation?
83. Have you both spent a lot of time alone together?
84. Does the person like to do special things to please himself/herself?
85. Does he/she get more gratification out of pleasing you?
86. Is the person selfish?
87. Are you selfish?
88. Does he/she have a very physically demanding job?
89. Do you seem to have more time on your hands than he/she does?
90. Does the person take a lot of business trips?
91. Does the person frequently go out with his/her co-workers?
92. Do you socialize a lot with your co-workers outside of the office?
93. Is flirting one of your favorite pastimes?
94. Do you like to have members of the opposite sex pay attention to you?
95. When on a date, do you ever pay?
96. Does the person pay attention to himself/herself with garish jewelry or loud clothes?
97. Do you like to dress conservatively?
98. Do you both like eating the same types of foods?
99. Do you think your intended mate is perfect?
100. Do you think he/she feels you're perfect?

QUIZ 13

What Are Your Core Issues?

Everyone has certain strong beliefs that aren't subject to compromise. These may involve religion, politics or personal needs. And no matter how deeply you feel you love someone, these beliefs can't be given up.

These, then, are your core issues. And it would be a good idea to put them down on paper before going on to the next quiz.

That way, when you start examining your differences in Quiz 14, you'll know instantly how serious a problem you could run into with your potential mate.

For example, children could be a core issue. You may hate them while your spouse longs for a large family. Will both of you ever be able to satisfactorily settle this issue? Not very likely.

Or you and your potential spouse may both want children. But one partner is significantly older than the other and may not be around to help raise them. Again, this could cause a significant problem.

On the other hand, if neither of you feels strongly about parenting, but one gets furious when the other starts to talk about his/her political views, this may be the core issue that needs looking into.

Climate can create a problem, if you long to live among the cool snow-capped mountain peaks while your mate wants to languish on a beach in Tahiti.

And even if it never became that extreme, how would both of you regulate the temperatures in an apartment if one likes it hot and the other cold.

Different food tastes may seem a simple enough problem now, but it could end up with you spending most of your married life in the kitchen. And if you don't like the idea of lingering over a hot stove, cooking his and hers, this particular person may not be your cup of tea.

So make a list of all the things you feel take top priority in your life on the following numbered lines.

Perhaps you have a few interests or perhaps many. But once you write them down (and this may be the first time you've thought about it), the results can be quite revealing.

1. ______________________________
2. ______________________________
3. ______________________________
4. ______________________________
5. ______________________________
6. ______________________________
7. ______________________________
8. ______________________________
9. ______________________________
10. ______________________________
11. ______________________________
12. ______________________________
13. ______________________________
14. ______________________________
15. ______________________________

QUIZ 14

How Much Difference Can You Tolerate?

When reading through the following questions, check the ones you think could lead to problems in a marriage.

Because these are personal feelings that even your friends and family might not know about, only you can judge how seriously they would affect your relationship.

When taking the quiz, answer the questions with your *first* impressions. And don't try to make yourself or your intended be what you think he/she should be. Take your time. You may be surprised at what you find out.

THE MARRIAGE CHECKLIST II

1. Is the person significantly older than you?
2. Is the person significantly younger than you?
3. Is he/she more educated than you?

4. Is he/she less educated than you?
5. Does he/she make more money than you do?
6. Does he/she make less money than you do?
7. Does the person have a lot of energy and stamina?
8. Is he/she always complaining of fatigue?
9. Are you both the same religion?
10. Are you of differing religions?
11. Do you share similar political views?
12. Are your political views vastly different?
13. Do you have the same cultural tastes?
14. Do you feel your potential mate is mostly interested in noncultural events?
15. Do you feel you are more intelligent than your potential mate?
16. Do you feel less intelligent than your potential mate?
17. Are your family backgrounds similar?
18. Are your family backgrounds very different?
19. Are you at your best during the early A.M. hours?
20. Does he/she only come alive at night?
21. Do you want to have children?
22. Does he/she dislike children?
23. Are you interested in pursuing a career?
24. Does he/she have career aspirations that would conflict?
25. Are you overly confident?
26. Is he/she insecure?
27. Do you feel that anything goes sexually as long as it makes you feel good?
28. Is the person's sexual behavior more conservative?
29. Are you dissatisfied with each other as sexual partners?
30. Are you able to fulfill each other's sexual needs?
31. Do you need to be impeccably groomed at all times?
32. Does he/she wear the first thing pulled out of the laundry basket?
33. Are you fashion-conscious and dressed in the latest styles?
34. Does the person still wear the clothes that he/she wore in college?
35. Is he/she always late?
36. Are you always on time?
37. Is your overall health good?
38. Does the person always complain about minor aches and pains?
39. Do you wish you could be five pounds thinner, or two inches taller, etc.?
40. Is the person satisfied with his/her body image?
41. Do you like to have fun?
42. Is the person serious-minded?
43. Do you love your job?
44. Is he/she dissatisfied with work?
45. Do you have any irrational fears?
46. Is the person untroubled by most things?
47. Do you have a great need for demonstrations of affection?
48. Is he/she embarrassed by physical displays of affection in public?
49. Are you in the mood for sex most of the time?
50. Does he/she feel sex should be restricted to only specific times?
51. Do you feel you have a great capacity for love?
52. Is he/she cold and unaffectionate?
53. Do you get jealous very easily?

54. Does the person do things to deliberately provoke your jealousy?
55. Is the person a flirt?
56. Does his/her bathroom etiquette leave something to be desired?
57. Does the person object to being controlled?
58. Do you have a high degree of self-esteem?
59. Does the person have a high degree of self-esteem?
60. Are you a creative person?
61. Does the person have any creative talents?
62. How important to you is self-expression?
63. Does the person feel that all sensitive persons are kooks?
64. Would you go crazy living in a small town?
65. Does the person prefer living in suburbia?
66. Does the person have health problems that would restrict areas where you could live?
67. Does the person have health problems that would restrict your lifestyle?
68. Is this person generally the life of the party?
69. Are you a wallflower?
70. Do you enjoy reading the same books and seeing the same movies?
71. Is the person an adventurer?
72. Do you dislike smokers?
73. Does this person have any habits that would upset you?
74. Do you dislike drinkers?
75. Do you have a drinking problem that might upset him?
76. Does roughing it mean to you a hotel without a color T.V.?
77. Does the person like to camp out?
78. Do you both like eating gourmet foods?
79. Does the person have special food or dietary needs?
80. Are you interested in physical fitness?
81. Is the person very body-conscious?
82. Is the person overweight?
83. Does the person come close to your preferences for body-type and hair color?
84. Are you well traveled?
85. Do you generally keep your things neat and orderly?
86. Do you like to impress strangers by putting on false airs once in a while?
87. Do you only like people who are down-to-earth?
88. In your opinion, what is the most important quality a husband/wife should have?
89. Does the person have this quality?
90. Do you always have to be on the go?
91. Does the person like to spend a lot of time at home?
92. Does the person complain of boredom a great deal?
93. Is the person easygoing and laid back?
94. Do you like doing everything by the book?
95. Does he/she like flaunting the rules once in a while?
96. Does the person respect you for your accomplishments?
97. Do you admire the person for things he/she has done?
98. Does he/she listen to you?
99. Do you like to take advice from others?
100. Were you originally attracted to each other because your tastes, experiences and cultural backgrounds were vastly different?

QUIZ 15

How Much Excitement Do You Need in Your Life?

1. Do you like to go exploring by yourself when in a strange city?
   (a) yes (b) sometimes (c) no

2. Do you have trouble accepting what other people tell you without first checking it out for yourself?
   (a) yes (b) sometimes (c) no

3. When having lunch with your co-workers, are you always the first one to finish?
   (a) yes (b) depends (c) no

4. Is a quiet evening at home with friends one of your favorite activities?
   (a) no (b) seldom (c) yes

5. Are you the type to speak your mind rather than hold things back?
   (a) yes (b) usually (c) no

6. Do you like people whom you think are less intelligent than you?
   (a) no (b) seldom (c) maybe

7. Do you have very specific goals in life you would like to attain?
   (a) yes (b) depends (c) no

8. If you could have lived in another time, would you have liked to have been an explorer?
   (a) yes (b) depends (c) no

9. Would it frighten you to speak in front of a group without first being prepared?
   (a) no (b) sometimes (c) yes

10. Do you like going to museums on Sunday afternoons?
    (a) no (b) depends (c) yes

11. Do you enjoy unpredictable things happening in your life?
    (a) yes (b) sometimes (c) no

12. Do you get bored taking vacations where you can only relax?
    (a) yes (b) sometimes (c) no

13. Do you have trouble finding something to do when you're alone?
    (a) no (b) sometimes (c) yes

14. Do you often get depressed because you're not as popular as you'd like to be?
    (a) no (b) seldom (c) yes

15. At work, do you play it safe and do the job the way you've always done it, even though you see a new way that could save time?
    (a) no (b) depends (c) yes

16. Do you admire people who think the way you do?
    (a) yes (b) usually (c) no

17. Are you a very outwardly expressive person?
    (a) yes (b) depends (c) no

18. Do you ever gamble on the stock market?
    (a) yes (b) depends (c) no

19. Do you like to go shopping alone, because you only trust your own taste?
    (a) yes (b) depends (c) no

20. Have you always dreamed of owning your own business?
    (a) yes (b) sometimes (c) no

21. Even though you have the money to travel, do you feel there's nothing better than staying in your own backyard?
    (a) no (b) seldom (c) yes

22. Are you often afraid to try something new, because you don't like looking awkward or silly?
    (a) no (b) seldom (c) yes

23. Do you like doing new things simply for the challenge?
    (a) yes (b) depends (c) no

24. Do you usually believe what other people tell you?
    (a) no (b) depends (c) yes

25. Are you easily influenced by your co-workers?
    (a) no (b) depends (c) yes

26. Do you feel you can let yourself go in a strange place where no one knows you?
    (a) yes (b) depends (c) no

27. Do you often change around the furniture in your apartment?
    (a) yes (b) sometimes (c) no

28. Do you follow fads?
    (a) no (b) depends (c) yes

29. Would you wear an outlandish outfit to a party, simply to attract attention?
    (a) yes (b) depends (c) no

30. Would you be a good candidate for assertiveness training?
    (a) no (b) depends (c) yes

QUIZ 16

What Kind of Lover Are You?

1. Would you marry someone because of his position?
   (a) yes (b) don't know (c) no

2. Do you look at relationships as fun things and never expect them to go anywhere?
   (a) sometimes (b) yes (c) no

3. When you fall in love with someone, would you like it to last forever?
   (a) don't know (b) no (c) yes

4. Could you love someone for his/her money?
   (a) yes (b) don't know (c) no

5. Does love last only as long as you want it to?
   (a) sometimes (b) yes (c) no

6. Would you like to find the kind of perfect love that poets write about?
   (a) maybe (b) no (c) yes

7. Do you see love as a game to be played, constantly proving you're the winner?
   (a) don't know (b) yes (c) no

8. Are you usually attracted to people in power?
   (a) yes (b) sometimes (c) no

9. Do you think being ready to fall in love is the key to finding a mate?
   (a) don't know (b) no (c) yes

10. Could you only fall in love with someone who was from an appropriate background like yours?
    (a) yes (b) don't know (c) no

11. Do you like having a lot of relationships in your life?
    (a) don't know (b) yes (c) no

12. Would you have to be in love with someone to marry them?
    (a) don't know (b) no (c) yes

13. Would you ever marry for any reason besides love?
    (a) yes (b) don't know (c) no

14. Do you think that a marriage for any other reason besides love would work out?
    (a) yes (b) maybe (c) no

15. Do you believe the only way you're ever going to achieve total happiness within yourself is through marriage and the special relationships you'll have with another person?
    (a) no (b) maybe (c) yes

16. Would you marry someone because he/she would be beneficial to your carrer?
    (a) yes (b) don't know (c) no

17. Do you enjoy flirting with people?
    (a) maybe (b) yes (c) don't know

18. Would you be able to judge on a first date whether you could fall in love or not?
    (a) no (b) maybe (c) yes

19. Do you often fantasize about how your true love will look?
    (a) no (b) sometimes (c) yes

20. Would you spend time dating someone you weren't emotionally involved with?
    (a) yes (b) sometimes (c) no

21. When on a date with someone new, would you be embarrassed when running into a former lover?
    (a) depends (b) no (c) yes

22. Would you be easily hurt if someone paid attention to your date?
    (a) depends (b) no (c) yes

23. Do you think flirting is appropriate behavior?
    (a) depends (b) yes (c) no

24. Are you usually attracted to a person because of the way he/she looks?
    (a) no (b) sometimes (c) yes

25. Do you feel that good sex in marriage is sometimes related to your feelings of financial security?
    (a) yes (b) depends (c) no

QUIZ 17

How Does Sex Rate in Your Life?

1. Are you satisfied with your partner in your current relationship?
   (a) yes (b) don't know (c) no

2. Do you wish he/she would be more romantic toward you?
   (a) no (b) don't know (c) yes

3. Is it easy for you to talk about your sexual preferences with your partner during lovemaking?
   (a) yes (b) sometimes (c) no

4. Do you find that most of the time you're the one to initiate sex with your partner?
   (a) no (b) don't know (c) yes

5. If you were displeased with something your partner did during lovemaking, would you tell him/her about it?
   (a) yes (b) sometimes (c) no

6. Do you feel talking during lovemaking ruins the feeling of romance?
   (a) no (b) don't know (c) yes

7. Do you fantasize during lovemaking?
   (a) sometimes (b) always (c) never

8. Would you ever withhold sex as a way to punish your partner?
   (a) no (b) maybe (c) yes

9. If you were not in the mood for sex, would you have it to please your partner?
   (a) sometimes (b) always (c) never

10. Do you find there are times when you're more in the mood for sex than others?
    (a) yes (b) no (c) don't know

11. Do you and your mate share the same sense of humor when it comes to sex?
    (a) yes (b) often (c) no

12. Are there certain sexual activities you would not allow your mate to engage in with you?
    (a) yes (b) maybe (c) no

13. Would you be willing to try anything to please your partner?
    (a) yes (b) don't know (c) no

14. Would you describe your lovemaking as repetitious?
    (a) no (b) sometimes (c) yes

15. Do you like to change positions and locations to make your sexual activities more exciting?
    (a) yes (b) don't know (c) no

16. Do you and your mate kiss a lot during lovemaking?
    (a) yes (b) seldom (c) no

17. Following orgasm would you like or allow your partner to continue caressing you and talking to you?
    (a) yes (b) seldom (c) no

18. Do erotic films, stories and art stimulate you sexually?
    (a) yes (b) sometimes (c) no

19. Does your partner get sexually excited by the same types of external cues as you do, i.e. soft lights, good music?
    (a) yes (b) seldom (c) no

20. Do you like making love only with the lights out?
    (a) no (b) depends (c) yes

21. Does your partner continually surprise you with new sexual demands?
    (a) no (b) seldom (c) yes

22. Does your partner know what it takes to turn you on?
    (a) yes (b) don't know (c) no

23. Do you like to spend a lot of time with your partner in foreplay?
    (a) yes (b) sometimes (c) no

24. Are you easily ready for sex?
    (a) yes (b) seldom (c) no

25. Do you wish you could be as free and uninhibited as your partner during sex?
    (a) no (b) maybe (c) yes

26. If you were going to choose a partner right now, would the person's sexual attractiveness be an important factor?
    (a) yes (b) maybe (c) no

27. Do you like to use personal aphrodisiacs to make sex a pleasurable experience for you?
    (a) sometimes (b) never (c) always

28. Can you only enjoy sex in familiar surroundings?
    (a) no (b) don't know (c) yes

29. Do you feel let down after making love because your partner was too quick or inattentive to your needs?
    (a) seldom (b) often (c) yes

30. Do you like engaging in sex just as a means of releasing physical tension?
    (a) sometimes (b) always (c) never

QUIZ 18

Do You Want to Be a Parent?

1. Do you think your current love interest would make a good parent?
   (a) yes (b) maybe (c) no

2. Does your potential spouse become impatient around children?
   (a) no (b) depends (c) yes

3. When visiting married friends, do you and your partner get actively involved in playing with their children?
   (a) yes (b) depends (c) no

4. Do you and your potential mate agree on the way you'd like to raise your children?
   (a) yes (b) sometimes (c) no

5. Would your mate like to have children?
   (a) yes (b) depends (c) no

6. Do you feel the presence of children in your life would fill a void that nothing else could?
   (a) yes (b) maybe (c) no

7. Do you think having children will be a means of guaranteeing security in your old age?
   (a) maybe (b) yes (c) no

8. Do you feel even though your partner isn't interested in having children now, his/her feelings would change later on?
   (a) no (b) depends (c) yes

9. Do you feel you could not love a person if he/she could not give you children?
   (a) no (b) depends (c) yes

10. Would you like to start a family immediately after getting married?
   (a) depends (b) maybe (c) no

11. Would you like to delay the start of a family until you and your mate have had a chance to grow in your careers?
   (a) depends (b) no (c) yes

12. Are you ready to devote the time and energy it takes to raise a child?
   (a) yes (b) maybe (c) no

13. Are you a person that's capable of sharing?
   (a) yes (b) sometimes (c) no

14. Can you picture yourself and your mate as parents?
   (a) yes (b) sometimes (c) no

15. Do you have any preconceived idea of what size family you'd like to have?
   (a) somewhat (b) no preference (c) very specific

To Be Answered if You Are a Male

QUIZ 19

What Do Men Expect Out of Marriage?

1. Are you shocked at the thought of a woman who doesn't want to have children?
   (a) yes (b) depends (c) no

2. Do you find dependency an attractive quality in a woman?
   (a) yes (b) depends (c) no

3. If married, would you feel intimidated if your wife made more money than you did?
   (a) yes (b) maybe (c) no

4. Do you feel after working all day you shouldn't be expected to help around the house?
   (a) yes (b) depends (c) no

5. Would you encourage your spouse to get involved in activities outside the home?
   (a) no (b) depends (c) yes

6. Would you get angry if your spouse made a decision about repairing the house without first consulting you?
   (a) yes (b) depends (c) no

7. Would you mind if your spouse kept a separate checking account?
   (a) yes (b) usually (c) no

8. If your wife liked the mountains and you liked the shore, would you consider taking separate vacations once in a while?
   (a) no (b) depends (c) yes

9. Do you feel boys and girls should perform the same chores around the house?
   (a) no (b) depends (c) yes

10. Do you get upset when your spouse is too tired at the end of the day to make love with you?
    (a) yes (b) usually (c) no

11. Do you expect your spouse to make a special effort to entertain when your family comes to visit?
    (a) yes (b) often (c) no

12. Would you refuse to allow your wife to go on a business trip with a male co-worker?
    (a) yes (b) usually (c) no

13. Do you feel it's the woman's role to bring up the children?
    (a) yes (b) depends (c) no

14. Do you feel it's a good idea to help your spouse with the housework once in a while?
    (a) maybe (b) no (c) yes

15. Do you think it's all right to keep certain financial information from your spouse because she wouldn't understand?
    (a) yes (b) sometimes (c) no

To Be Answered if You Are a Female

QUIZ 20

What Do Women Expect Out of Marriage?

1. Do you think the best way women can develop their full potential is by being good wives and mothers?
   (a) yes (b) depends (c) no

2. Do you feel it's still very difficult for a single woman to get ahead in today's society?
   (a) yes (b) depends (c) no

3. Do you think a woman who entrusts her children to a day-care center is being irresponsible?
   (a) yes (b) depends (c) no

4. Do you think you can have a career and raise a child at the same time?
   (a) no (b) seldom (c) yes

5. If married, would you expect your mate to share the household and parenting duties as equally as possible?
   (a) no (b) usually (c) yes

6. Do you feel the female role in marriage is to cook, keep house and care for the children?
   (a) yes (b) depends (c) no

7. Do you think that children of different sexes should be brought up the same way?
   (a) no (b) depends (c) yes

8. If you were employed before marriage, would you give up your job if asked to do so by your mate?
   (a) yes (b) depends (c) no

9. Would it bother you if your spouse had an impressive job title?
   (a) no (b) depends (c) yes

10. Do you feel in a marriage either partner, depending on their strengths and weaknesses, can perform any number of household duties?
    (a) no (b) maybe (c) yes

11. Do you feel the husband's role in marriage is to be the main breadwinner and do minor chores around the house?
    (a) yes (b) depends (c) no

12. Do you feel it's all right to have a night out with your friends once in a while?
    (a) no (b) depends (c) yes

13. If both spouses worked, would you still feel only the husband should be in charge of the budget and bill paying?
    (a) yes (b) depends (c) yes

14. Do you feel any decisions regarding the family should be made by both partners?
    (a) no (b) usually (c) yes

15. Would you feel secure at the thought of someone taking care of you and providing for your welfare?
    (a) yes (b) depends (c) no

QUIZ 21

Are You Ready to Share Your Life with Someone?

1. Do you have mixed feelings about marriage because you fear giving up your freedom?
   (a) never (b) sometimes (c) always

2. Do you like to engage in a lot of activities with your friends?
   (a) sometimes (b) usually (c) rarely

3. Would you rather spend time on your hobbies than be out partying with friends?
   (a) no (b) sometimes (c) yes

4. Do you like to mutually discuss things with your friends before you decide what you're going to do?
   (a) usually (b) rarely (c) sometimes

5. At work, do people get on your nerves if they're around you a lot?
   (a) no (b) depends (c) yes

6. Are friendships very important in your life?
   (a) yes (b) depends (c) no

7. Do you staunchly hold on to your own opinions even when others are against you?
   (a) depends (b) rarely (c) frequently

8. Would you love the freedom of being alone in a strange city?
   (a) no (b) don't know (c) yes

9. Do you need to ask other people's opinions before you make a decision?
   (a) yes (b) sometimes (c) no

10. If married, would you object to handing over your paycheck to your spouse?
    (a) no (b) depends (c) yes

11. Would you ever be the first one in your group to voice an unpopular opinion?
    (a) no (b) depends (c) yes

12. Would you rather be comfortable and wear what you liked than keep up with the latest styles in clothes?
    (a) yes (b) usually (c) no

13. If you're involved in an argument and have to defend certain principles you believe in, would you stick to your guns no matter what?
    (a) frequently (b) usually (c) always

14. Would you avoid buying a hat that you really liked because none of your friends wore hats?
    (a) yes (b) maybe (c) no

15. If you're in a restaurant and your date suggests food you're not particularly fond of, would you make some excuse and order what you liked instead?
    (a) no (b) probably (c) yes

Scoring Instructions for Part Two

Rating

The ten quizzes in Part Two are designed to do the following:

1) Help you pinpoint your perfect mate.
2) Rate your attitudes on key marriage issues.
3) Show you how to select the most compatible person for your needs.

Scoring

In Quizzes 12, 13, and 14, there are no right or wrong answers. These are simply meant to be checklists of qualities or characteristics that only you can rate, based on how they fit into your life, or how you feel about things in general.

As a means of comparison, you could set a value of 1 for all the characteristics that *do* please you about a person, and a 0 for the ones that *don't*. That way you would have a numerical score to evaluate your decision, particularly if you already have a special person in mind.

Quizzes 15 through 21 are to be scored. To change your answers to these questions into numerical values, do as follows:

1) For each (a) answer—give yourself 3 points.
2) For each (b) answer—give yourself 2 points.
3) For each (c) answer—give yourself 1 point.

Then total up the number of points you have for each quiz.

Evaluating

An explanation will be given at the beginning of each quiz on how your attitudes will affect the choice of a future mate. Then, based on your score values and the range into which they fit, you will be given pointers on how to select the most compatible partner for your needs.

QUIZ 15
How Much Excitement Do You Need in Your Life?

Everyone experiences varying degrees of activity and stimulation in their lives. And these can differ considerably for each person.

These differences may not matter when you are single because you can pick from a wide selection of friends for the right partner to fit a particular mood or occasion.

Being married, however, is a different story, especially if you and your partner don't have the same need for excitement.

If you scored between:

76–90 If you score high in this category, and choose a mate who scores low, you'd bore each other to tears before the honeymoon was over.

51–75 Lucky you. Your score is in the middle, and you can most likely adapt to either a high-stimulation seeker or a low-stimulation sleeper.

30–50 A low-stimulation personality like yours is fine, as long as you stay with your own kind. Playing out of your league could create stress in a relationship.

QUIZ 16
What Kind of Lover Are You?

There are several ways to look at love. You can be totally practical about it. You can play a game with it. Or you can romanticize it, the way poets do. And by knowing what kind of lover you are, you can understand your behavior a lot more, especially if you're not doing too well in the area of personal relationships.

If you scored between:

56–75 You're a logical, practical lover who's interested in what a relationship can do for you. And you'd expect a marriage mate to fit the same criteria.

40–55 You like to play at love and find it hard to take a relationship seriously. Even though you may have other good qualifications for marriage, this attitude would put marrying out of the picture for you for a while.

25–39 You're a romantic. You believe in love at first sight. You're in love with love. And lots of people can seem right. You have to balance your capacity for love with much more logic.

QUIZ 17
How Does Sex Rate in Your Life?

Sex is crucial to a happy marriage. It can become a problem if one partner takes pride in being a sexual athlete in the bedroom, while the other would rather be in the kitchen baking biscuits. It's important to try to match up with someone who is as interested in sex as you are.

If you scored between:

71–90 If there were trophies for sex, you'd receive one.

51–70 You truly enjoy sex, but there are times when you can take it or leave it.

30–50 Sex is not a priority in your life. Possibly your job or other responsibilities are so draining that you don't have the energy left for it. However, your attitude could change in the future.

QUIZ 18
Do You Want to Be a Parent?

Your views on parenting are important. And these should always be discussed with a potential mate before marriage; otherwise, problems and resentments will surface later on.

If you scored between:

35–45 You truly love and want children, and would feel something missing in your life without them.

25–34 Having children and a family is one priority in your life, but not the most important one.

15–24 Forget about parenting, as you're probably not the type.

QUIZ 19
What Do Men Expect Out of Marriage?

The point here is to determine whether you're a traditionalist or a modernist in your thinking about marriage and the duties of a spouse. While neither attitude will make or break a marriage, it's thinking alike that promises the most successful union.

If you scored between:

35–45 Your attitudes about marriage are the old-fashioned kind. You expect a wife to tend to home and hearth while you're out battling the world for the family's financial security.

25–34 You're a middle-of-the-roader. You'd let your wife work if she wanted to, and make some arrangements to share household duties. But you still feel the responsibility of the home should be on her shoulders.

15–24 You're an egalitarian. It doesn't matter who does what around the house. You feel it should be divided according to who has the most talent for the particular task, even when it comes down to changing the baby's diapers.

QUIZ 20
What Do Women Expect Out of Marriage?

As in Quiz 19, the point here is to determine whether you're a traditionalist or a modernist in your thinking about marriage and the duties of a spouse. While neither attitude is right or wrong, it's thinking alike that promises the most successful union.

If you scored between:

35–45 You're definitely the old-fashioned kind. Your family would be your career, and their creature comforts your first and foremost priority. You would not expect your husband to be involved in the home, because that's your turf. But you would expect him to support you and provide for your needs.

25–34 You want a career and a family. You expect your mate to share in the household duties as well as the raising of children. And you wouldn't hesitate to rely on outside help if it were necessary.

15–24 You definitely think like a modernist, if not quite a superwoman. You want to keep some independence. Although married with a home and family, you would never neglect doing the things that made you happy.

QUIZ 21
Are You Ready to Share Your Life with Someone?

Giving up your independence for marriage is a tough issue to face. Just how ready are you?

If you scored between:

35–45 You would have no problem giving up your independence to marry.

25–34 For you this is an uncomfortable choice to make. But when the time comes, you will be able to do it, perhaps with just a tinge of fear.

15–24 Right now, forget about marriage. You're too independent to be able to comfortably share your life with someone. But it doesn't mean that you won't think differently sometime in the future.

HOW DO YOU FEEL ABOUT YOUR MARRIAGE?

PART Three

HOW DO YOU FEEL ABOUT YOUR MARRIAGE? Is it as good as you'd like it to be? Or is it even better than your wildest dreams?

Whatever your answer, you can find out just how well matched you and your spouse really are after you take the following eighteen quizzes.

This section is designed to help you determine the well-being of your marriage by examining the different aspects of your life together.

You will gain new insights into your mate's personality as well as your own; you'll be able to look at the overall relationship to see how it's functioning; also you'll find out if there are trouble spots that need special attention.

Then you and your spouse can put the information to practical use, by strengthening the weak areas and making the strong ones even more satisfying.

It's a good idea for you and your spouse to take the quizzes together, using separate answer sheets. After you've finished totaling your scores (scoring will be explained at the end of this section), you can compare your answers and find out some very revealing truths.

Answer each quiz question as you feel it applies to your moods. If you're not sure of a response, answer as closely to your true feelings as you can.

Don't think of these quizzes as a pass-or-fail situation; instead, treat them as eye openers. They can show you what's already good about your marriage and also help you to begin talking to each other about the unseen problems that affect your relationship.

Spouses, no matter how close, often keep whole reservoirs of feelings bottled up inside that are never revealed to each other.

Taking these quizzes may help to open up feelings hidden away for a long time, and allow each of you to get to know the secret side of the other.

Best of all, it can be the beginning of renewed love for each other.

QUIZ 22

How Does Sex Rate in Your Marriage?

1. Is it difficult for you to talk to your partner about your sexual hang-ups?
   (a) no (b) sometimes (c) yes

2. Are you satisfied with the regularity of sex in your marriage?
   (a) yes (b) usually (c) no

3. Beside it being a physical release, do you enjoy sex because it's fun?
   (a) yes (b) very often (c) no

4. After an enjoyable night of sex, do you feel better and happier the next day?
   (a) yes (b) usually (c) rarely

5. Do you have a definite pattern of sexual activity?
   (a) no (b) usually (c) yes

6. Do you get upset when separated from your spouse because you have to alter this pattern?
   (a) no (b) sometimes (c) yes

7. Does sex always have to be the way you want it to be?
   (a) no (b) usually (c) yes

8. Do you initiate the sexual activity as often as your spouse?
   (a) yes (b) maybe (c) no

9. Do you feel you can refuse to have sex without upsetting your spouse?
   (a) yes (b) sometimes (c) no

10. Do you look forward to having sex with your partner?
    (a) yes (b) rarely (c) no

11. Do you often think about your spouse in a sexual way?
    (a) often (b) sometimes (c) seldom

12. Do you feel marriage deprives you of adventures and pleasures you'd have as a single person?
    (a) rarely (b) sometimes (c) often

13. Do you ever find yourself wishing that you could have an affair?
    (a) no (b) rarely (c) often

14. Do you appreciate married sex mostly because it promises the continuity of sex with a beloved partner?
    (a) yes (b) maybe (c) no

15. Do you think one of the greatest advantages of marriage is the promise of long-term commitment and companionship?
    (a) yes (b) sometimes (c) no

16. Do you find you like to fantasize a lot while making love with your partner?
    (a) rarely (b) sometimes (c) often

17. Would you say that sex in your marriage is as good as you'd like to to be?
    (a) yes (b) don't know (c) no

18. Do you know what it takes to arouse your partner sexually?
    (a) yes (b) maybe (c) no

19. Does your partner know what parts of your body, when stimulated, bring you the most pleasure?
    (a) yes (b) maybe (c) no

20. Would you like your mate to spend more time in foreplay?
    (a) sometimes (b) often (c) usually

21. If your mate reaches orgasm before you do, would he/she continue stimulating you until you reach orgasm?
    (a) yes (b) depends (c) no

22. Would your partner be turned off by having sex in strange surroundings?
    (a) no (b) depends (c) yes

23. Do you often feel that sex is all your mate ever thinks about?
(a) no (b) maybe (c) yes

24. At the end of a heated argument, would you be able to make love with your partner?
(a) maybe (b) rarely (c) no

25. Do you feel that sex is more than a means of releasing physical tension?
(a) yes (b) don't know (c) no

QUIZ 23

What Are the Sexual Trouble Spots in Your Marriage?

1. Does your interest in sex diminish if you've had a trying week at work?
(a) sometimes (b) usually (c) often

2. Do you find your current sexual activity is too infrequent to be fulfilling?
(a) no (b) maybe (c) yes

3. Does your job keep you away from home for long periods of time?
(a) no (b) sometimes (c) yes

4. Have you thought about having an affair because in your marriage you're alone so much of the time?
(a) no (b) not seriously (c) occasionally

5. When you have to spend any prolonged period of time away from your spouse, do you try to keep in as close contact as possible with frequent phone calls, letters and gifts?
(a) always (b) sometimes (c) not really

6. Do you feel like making love when your spouse doesn't?
(a) sometimes (b) occasionally (c) usually

7. Do you feel rejected when your spouse is too tired after work to want to make love?
(a) sometimes (b) usually (c) often

8. Would you describe yourself as a physically affectionate person?
(a) yes (b) sometimes (c) not much

9. Do you get uncomfortable and even angry when your spouse encourages you to make love in unfamiliar surroundings?
(a) sometimes (b) usually (c) always

10. How would you rate your sex life over the past year?
(a) terrific (b) good (c) adequate

11. Have you noted a change in your sexual relations over the last year?
(a) it's increased (b) it's stayed the same (c) it's decreased

12. Do you withhold sex when you're angry with your spouse?
(a) rarely (b) sometimes (c) always

13. Do you find you're so busy with your community work that you have very little time left for sex?
    (a) rarely (b) sometimes (c) often

14. Do you like sex to be romantic, à la Romeo and Juliet, while your mate prefers a more direct approach, something like Tarzan and Jane?
    (a) yes (b) maybe (c) no

15. Do you feel there's a level of intimacy yet to be achieved with your spouse, although you've been married for a while?
    (a) yes (b) maybe (c) no

16. If you found out your mate was involved in an affair, would you leave the marriage?
    (a) depends (b) probably (c) definitely

17. Do you often feel that your spouse is too sexually demanding?
    (a) no (b) occasionally (c) yes

18. Do you have very definite ideas about what is normal and correct in sex?
    (a) no (b) maybe (c) yes

19. Do you make as much of an effort to please your spouse now as in the past?
    (a) just as much (b) not as much (c) rarely

20. Would you use sex to prove your masculinity or feminity?
    (a) sometimes (b) never (c) always

21. Do you deny your spouse sex when you're not in the mood?
    (a) sometimes (b) frequently (c) always

22. Do you like to have sex because it makes you feel better about yourself?
    (a) yes (b) usually (c) no

23. Do you often wish you could be as sexually expressive as your spouse?
    (a) sometimes (b) frequently (c) always

24. Do you find when your partner is away for any length of time that you think about having sex with someone else?
    (a) rarely (b) sometimes (c) frequently

25. Do you feel you and your spouse are about equally matched in your sexual drives?
    (a) yes (b) maybe (c) no

26. Do you feel that sexually you have a lot more to give than your spouse demands?
    (a) no (b) maybe (c) yes

27. Are you amazed at the 1980s attitudes toward sex?
    (a) sometimes (b) usually (c) always

28. If there are family problems, does your sexual performance suffer?
    (a) rarely (b) sometimes (c) always

29. Do you go for weeks at a time without having sex with your spouse?
    (a) rarely (b) sometimes (c) frequently

30. When on vacation, can you capture those wild, crazy feelings you once had for your spouse?
    (a) often (b) sometimes (c) rarely

31. Do you and your spouse still neck and pet before sex?
    (a) often (b) occasionally (c) seldom

32. Would you say that sex is not as fulfilling to you as it used to be?
    (a) no (b) sometimes (c) often

33. Has your capacity for sex diminished, because of a health problem or because you're taking some kind of strong medication?
    (a) no (b) cannot tell (c) yes

34. Do you feel there would come a time in your relationship when you and your spouse could live together without sex?
    (a) no (b) don't know (c) yes

35. If you know that your partner has a particular sexual preference, do you make an effort to please?
    (a) always (b) sometimes (c) rarely

QUIZ 24

Do You and Your Mate Operate on the Same Wavelength?

1. Do you think a person must have three meals a day?
   (a) usually (b) frequently (c) always

2. Do you have to have eight hours of sleep each night?
   (a) if possible (b) mostly (c) absolutely

3. Can you grab a hot dog on the run and call it lunch?
   (a) if necessary (b) maybe (c) never

4. Does making love help you fall asleep?
   (a) often (b) sometimes (c) rarely

5. Are you the type of person who will go to a movie on the spur of the moment?
   (a) yes (b) rarely (c) no

6. Would you ever take a trip without first having made reservations at a hotel?
   (a) yes (b) maybe (c) no

7. Do you always keep a passport ready in the drawer, even though you've never been out of the country?
   (a) no (b) maybe (c) yes

8. Can you enjoy reading all kinds of books?
   (a) yes (b) somewhat (c) no

9. Do you get indigestion very easily?
   (a) no (b) depends on what you eat (c) yes

10. Would you refuse to go swimming in a friend's pool if you didn't have your own bathing suit?
   (a) no (b) maybe (c) yes

11. Could you be tempted to go dancing late at night when you heard of a new place?
   (a) yes (b) maybe (c) no

12. Are you the type of person to bound out of bed first thing in the morning?
   (a) yes (b) often (c) never

13. Can people only approach you after you've had your first cup of coffee in the morning?
   (a) no (b) sometimes (c) always

14. Would you be willing to try a restaurant you've never been to before?
   (a) yes (b) rarely (c) no

15. Is it hard for you to find the right moment to have sex?
   (a) no (b) rarely (c) usually

16. Do your feelings about your spouse change from time to time?
   (a) yes (b) sometimes (c) no

17. Do you get upset if your regular schedule is disrupted?
   (a) sometimes (b) frequently (c) always

18. Do you like shopping in certain stores because you know where everything is?
   (a) yes (b) maybe (c) depends

19. Would you be willing to try an ethnic food that you've never had before?
   (a) yes (b) maybe (c) no

20. Is it possible for you to have sex after doing something physically exerting?
   (a) often (b) sometimes (c) never

21. Do you like to play games as part of your lovemaking?
   (a) often (b) sometimes (c) rarely

22. Are there only certain movies that you enjoy?
   (a) no (b) maybe (c) yes

23. Does the decor of your bedroom affect your mood?
   (a) not easily (b) easily (c) very easily

24. Do you like the feeling of using creams, oils and lotions on your body?
   (a) sometimes (b) usually (c) often

25. Are you uncomfortable with new people?
(a) usually (b) not usually (c) rarely

26. Does it take you awhile to adjust to new surroundings?
(a) sometimes (b) usually (c) always

27. If someone played a practical joke on you, would you think it was funny?
(a) sometimes (b) rarely (c) never

28. If someone played a practical joke on you, would you be offended or embarrassed?
(a) maybe (b) probably (c) definitely

29. If you went on vacation and your hotel room didn't have a bathtub, would this upset you?
(a) no (b) unlikely (c) maybe

30. If you were having a party, and your child's pet hamster got loose among the guests, would you feel the evening was ruined?
(a) no (b) possibly (c) probably

31. Would you watch a pornographic movie with your mate?
(a) probably (b) maybe (c) no

32. If you went on vacation and your hotel offered a choice of regular or water beds, would you take the plunge and try something different?
(a) probably (b) maybe (c) unlikely

33. Do you like to do different things just for the excitement of the change?
(a) yes (b) sometimes (c) rarely

34. Do you have certain fears that keep you from doing a lot of things you'd like to do?
(a) no (b) a few (c) a lot

35. Would you read a sex manual to try to improve some of your bedroom techniques?
(a) yes (b) maybe (c) no

36. If you just won some skis in a contest, but never tried the sport before, would this perk up your interest?
(a) yes (b) probably (c) maybe

37. Does each new season give you a feeling of renewed vigor for what's ahead?
(a) yes (b) sometimes (c) depends

38. Are you the first person in your group to wear the most up-to-date clothes?
(a) sometimes (b) rarely (c) often

39. Would you try anything once?
(a) almost (b) maybe (c) no

40. Would you dress up in a costume as part of your lovemaking?
(a) maybe (b) don't know (c) no

QUIZ 25

Do You Have a Healthy Marriage?

1. Do you and your spouse try to do little things like exchanging love tokens for no special reason?
(a) yes (b) sometimes (c) no

2. Do you tell your spouse when he/she has done something especially pleasing for you?
(a) yes (b) usually (c) no

3. Does your marriage come first before life's many other demands?
(a) yes (b) sometimes (c) no

4. Would you fight as hard to make a success of your marriage as you do in your job?
(a) usually (b) sometimes (c) rarely

5. Do you and your spouse get involved in activities that you can both do together?
(a) yes (b) frequently (c) no

6. Is there any other relationship you have that makes you feel as satisfied and content as the one you have with your spouse?
(a) no (b) maybe (c) yes

7. Are you content to be in a long-term, intense relationship with your spouse?
(a) yes (b) often (c) no

8. Do you appreciate your spouse, whether things in life are going good or bad?
(a) yes (b) usually (c) no

9. Does your family's happiness and contentment come first before any other outside influence?
(a) yes (b) sometimes (c) no

10. Is your spouse also your best friend?
(a) yes (b) mostly (c) no

11. Do you find having a loving partner makes life easier to cope with?
(a) yes (b) usually (c) no

12. Would you describe your sex life together as very satisfying?
(a) yes (b) often (c) no

13. Even if you weren't particularly in the mood to make love, would you accommodate your partner if that's what your partner really wanted?
(a) yes (b) usually (c) no

14. Can you and your partner share your feelings easily with each other?
    (a) often (b) sometimes (c) rarely

15. Do you find that with each crisis your family's been through, you've grown closer together?
    (a) yes (b) maybe (c) no

16. Do you base your behavior on what people outside the family expect of you?
    (a) rarely (b) sometimes (c) usually

17. Do both you and your spouse have the same sexual needs?
    (a) often (b) sometimes (c) rarely

18. Do you and your spouse talk to each other about things that don't always involve family matters?
    (a) yes (b) often (c) rarely

19. Do you argue a lot with your spouse?
    (a) no (b) don't know (c) yes

20. Do you resolve your arguments quickly?
    (a) usually (b) sometimes (c) rarely

21. Would you ever try to manipulate your spouse to get what you wanted?
    (a) seldom (b) maybe (c) yes

22. No matter what you've both been through so far, do you still have a pretty optimistic attitude about life?
    (a) usually (b) sometimes (c) rarely

23. Do you and your spouse have similar religious convictions?
    (a) yes (b) up to a point (c) no

24. Do you agree that building a good, strong marriage takes a lot of work?
    (a) yes (b) sometimes (c) no

25. Do you feel that even though you're married, you should still maintain a certain amount of independence and set your own goals in life?
    (a) yes (b) depends (c) no

To Be Answered by Wives Only

QUIZ 26

What Do Wives Expect Out of Marriage?

1. Do you take pride in knowing that your home is as neat as a pin?
   (a) always (b) sometimes (c) rarely

2. Do you thoroughly enjoy spending a quiet evening at home while your spouse sits opposite reading the evening papers?
   (a) yes (b) sometimes (c) no

3. Do you have a sense of pride in what you do, even though a lot of your time is spent running errands?
   (a) sometimes (b) usually (c) rarely

4. Do you feel it's your responsibility to cook a good breakfast for the family every morning before they go off to start their day?
   (a) yes (b) depends (c) no

5. Were you eager to give up your job after marriage to take on the role of housewife?
   (a) yes (b) not sure (c) no

6. Would you reject any outside interests that would interfere with your being home to start dinner for your family?
   (a) yes (b) sometimes (c) no

7. Would you make any decision regarding the family without first consulting your husband?
   (a) no (b) depends (c) yes

8. Would you ever consider having an affair because you had a lot of time on your hands and it seemed like fun?
   (a) no (b) maybe (c) yes

9. Would you go to a social affair without your husband?
   (a) no (b) depends (c) yes

10. Do you think repair jobs around the house belong to your husband?
    (a) often (b) maybe (c) no

11. When going out for the evening, do you agree with what your husband wants to do?
    (a) yes (b) sometimes (c) no

12. Do you fantasize about being single?
    (a) rarely (b) sometimes (c) frequently

13. Does it matter if your children eat peanut butter and jelly sandwiches for lunch three days in a row?
    (a) yes (b) depends (c) no

14. When your husband starts complaining about his job, do you dutifully listen and sympathize?
    (a) yes (b) sometimes (c) no

15. When your husband starts complaining about his job, do you tell him he's got it easy, compared to your responsibilities?
    (a) rarely (b) sometimes (c) often

16. Do you look forward to your kids going away for sleep-over parties so that you can have some peace and quiet?
    (a) no (b) sometimes (c) yes

17. Do you still keep up friendships that your spouse may not approve of?
    (a) no (b) maybe (c) yes

18. If you took a job outside the home, do you believe that you and your spouse should share the household duties?
    (a) no (b) depends (c) yes

19. If you heard about one of your friends getting a divorce, would you feel a slight pang of envy at her freedom?
    (a) no (b) don't know (c) yes

20. Do you tell your spouse your troubles?
    (a) yes (b) maybe (c) no

21. Do you keep your own bank account?
    (a) no (b) would like to (c) yes

22. Would you ever take a trip or a vacation without your spouse?
    (a) no (b) would like to (c) yes

23. Do you dress to please your husband?
    (a) yes (b) sometimes (c) no

24. Would you let anyone into your home if it wasn't spotless?
    (a) no (b) depends (c) yes

25. Do you enjoy looking through recipe books, then driving around to several stores for the ingredients, just to prepare a good meal for your family?
    (a) yes (b) sometimes (c) no

To Be Answered by Husbands Only

QUIZ 27

What Do Husbands Expect Out of Marriage?

1. Do you encourage your wife to look over the family budget?
   (a) no (b) sometimes (c) yes

2. Do you think a man has a right to pursue his own interests outside the home?
   (a) yes (b) maybe (c) no

3. Do you expect your mate to stay within a budget which you set for family expenses?
   (a) yes (b) usually (c) no

4. Do you remember your spouse on her birthday, anniversary or other special occasions?
   (a) yes (b) sometimes (c) no

5. Do you object to sharing the household responsibilities with your mate even though you both work outside the house?
   (a) yes (b) quite often (c) no

6. If you're working overtime, do you think your wife should keep the dinner waiting?
   (a) yes (b) maybe (c) no

7. Do you like to spend an occasional night out with your friends, even though your wife feels that this takes time away from her?
   (a) yes (b) sometimes (c) no

8. Do you make an effort to be friendly with your wife's relatives?
   (a) yes (b) maybe (c) no

9. Do you feel that your sons and daughters should be brought up differently?
   (a) yes (b) maybe (c) no

10. Do you think a wife should be understanding when you have to bring work home?
    (a) yes (b) maybe (c) no

11. Do you think a wife should listen to what a husband has to say?
    (a) yes (b) sometimes (c) no

12. Would you like your mate to take more of an interest in sharing your hobbies?
    (a) yes (b) maybe (c) no

13. Do you resent your wife telling you not to see certain friends?
    (a) yes (b) sometimes (c) no

14. Do you pay as much attention to your clothes when you're at home as you do for work?
    (a) yes (b) not often (c) no

15. Do you think on the weekend you're entitled to more rest than your wife?
    (a) yes (b) maybe (c) no

16. Do you think men have a better sense of humor than women?
    (a) yes (b) maybe (c) depends

17. Do you help with the cooking?
    (a) no (b) sometimes (c) yes

18. Would it make you feel uncomfortable if your wife was earning more money than you?
    (a) yes (b) maybe (c) no

19. Do you ask your wife for financial advice?
    (a) no (b) sometimes (c) yes

20. How would you feel if your wife had more school degrees than you?
(a) uncomfortable (b) don't know (c) don't care

21. Do you argue with your mate in public?
(a) no (b) maybe (c) yes

22. Do you hold your wife responsible for the children's behavior?
(a) yes (b) often (c) no

23. Has your wife ever told you that she feels you have unreasonable expectations of her as a wife and mother?
(a) yes (b) sometimes (c) occasionally

24. When dining at home with your family, do you feel you can relax your table manners?
(a) no (b) depends (c) yes

25. Does your family come first as the most important priority?
(a) yes, always (b) depends (c) not always

QUIZ 28

Is Financial Stress Hurting Your Family?

1. If your spouse lost his/her job, would you blame him/her for the family's financial discomfort?
(a) no (b) maybe (c) yes

2. Would you blame yourself?
(a) no (b) maybe (c) yes

3. Would you sit down together to try to get the family back on its feet?
(a) yes (b) maybe (c) no

4. If you find the bills are getting completely out of hand because of your spouse's overspending, would you get angry at him/her?
(a) yes (b) usually (c) no

5. If you needed things for the house, would you expect your spouse to take a second job so you could afford them?
(a) sometimes (b) usually (c) yes

6. Would you take a second job to be able to afford them?
(a) yes (b) depends (c) no

7. Would you continue to have your own bank account even when married?
(a) no (b) maybe (c) yes

8. If you were overextended with bills, credit card charges and loans to family members and friends, would you consider taking one main consolidation loan as a way of getting out of debt?
(a) yes (b) depends (c) no

9. Do you buy only what you can pay cash for?
   (a) usually (b) sometimes (c) rarely

10. Have you held and quit several jobs in the past few years?
   (a) no (b) don't know (c) yes

11. Is it hard for you to get along well with your co-workers?
   (a) no (b) depends (c) yes

12. Do you often feel if you had enough money, life would be problem-free?
   (a) no (b) maybe (c) yes

13. If your neighbor got a new car, would you have to have one too, even though you knew you couldn't afford it?
   (a) no (b) maybe (c) yes

14. Do you like to impress your friends with your lavish parties and expensive clothes, even though this life-style keeps your family in a financial hole?
   (a) no (b) don't know (c) yes

15. Would you feel cheated if your spouse couldn't provide for you in a very lavish manner?
   (a) no (b) maybe (c) yes

16. Is the subject of money taboo in your marriage?
   (a) no (b) maybe (c) yes

17. Is it easier for you to talk to your spouse about your sexual preferences than about money?
   (a) no (b) depends (c) yes

18. Do you feel there's a lot you don't know about the way your family's finances are handled?
   (a) no (b) maybe (c) yes

19. Do you pay most of your bills with cash?
   (a) yes (b) sometimes (c) no

20. Do you buy most of your items with credit cards?
   (a) no (b) depends (c) yes

21. Are most of your bills paid on time?
   (a) yes (b) sometimes (c) no

22. If you're behind on some bills, do you at least try to make some type of small payments to keep your creditors happy?
   (a) yes (b) usually (c) no

23. Are you and your spouse budgeting now to buy a house in the future?
   (a) yes (b) does not apply (c) no

24. Do you and your spouse set priorities on the major items you would like to buy and then work this into your budget?
    (a) often (b) sometimes (c) rarely

25. Does your savings plan depend on whatever cash is left at the end of the month?
    (a) no (b) usually (c) yes

26. Have you and your spouse set up guidelines for spending money on clothing, vacations and other luxury items?
    (a) yes (b) maybe (c) no

27. Do you have a budget set up to cover emergency situations?
    (a) yes (b) maybe (c) no

28. Do you have a readily available list of all your insurance policies and investments?
    (a) yes (b) maybe (c) no

29. Have you and your spouse made out a will?
    (a) yes (b) we intend to (c) no

30. Even though you and your spouse make enough money to cover your monthly bills, do you seem to run short?
    (a) no (b) sometimes (c) yes

31. Do you or your spouse indulge in impulse spending?
    (a) rarely (b) sometimes (c) yes

32. Do you like to go shopping when you're depressed?
    (a) no (b) often (c) yes

33. Do you keep a record of all your major purchases?
    (a) yes (b) for some (c) no

34. Have you ever been seriously in debt in the past, prior to getting married?
    (a) no (b) don't know (c) yes

35. Judging by your past finances, do you ever think you might have to declare bankruptcy?
    (a) unlikely (b) maybe (c) likely

QUIZ 29

How Satisfying Is Your Marriage?

1. Do you feel you love your partner as much as he/she loves you?
   (a) yes (b) maybe (c) no

2. Have you and your spouse grown closer together since the beginning of your marriage?
   (a) yes (b) maybe (c) no

3. Has your marriage turned out to be everything you expected it to be?
   (a) mostly (b) sometimes (c) no

4. Do you feel that your marriage has failed to somehow live up to your expectations?
   (a) no (b) sometimes (c) yes

5. If you had the choice again, would you marry the same person?
   (a) of course (b) maybe (c) no

6. Do you kiss your spouse every day?
   (a) yes (b) usually (c) rarely

7. Are there problem areas in your marriage that you still find difficult to discuss with your spouse?
   (a) no (b) some (c) yes

8. Do you feel that the emotional security you get from being married makes it all worthwhile?
   (a) yes (b) usually (c) no

9. Do you feel that the sexual fulfillment you get from being married makes it all worthwhile?
   (a) yes (b) usually (c) no

10. Do you feel your loss of independence does not make the marriage state worthwhile?
   (a) no (b) rarely (c) yes

11. Are you satisfied with your spouse as a sexual partner?
   (a) yes (b) usually (c) no

12. Do you ever think about cheating on your spouse just for the thrill of something different?
   (a) rarely (b) occasionally (c) frequently

13. Have you ever been unfaithful to your spouse?
   (a) no (b) no comment (c) yes

14. Do you think your spouse has ever been unfaithful to you?
   (a) no (b) maybe (c) yes

15. Is it easy for you to name three qualities that you love about your spouse?
   (a) yes (b) usually (c) no

16. If you could turn your spouse into a different person right now, would you do it?
   (a) no (b) depends (c) yes

17. Has your spouse been able to live up to your early premarital expectations?
   (a) a lot (b) mostly (c) not lived up to them

18. Do you think you have lived up to your spouse's expectations?
    (a) I hope so (b) mostly (c) not lived up to them

19. When you think about your spouse, does it give you a feeling of contentment?
    (a) yes (b) usually (c) no

20. Do you feel lucky to be married to your spouse?
    (a) often (b) sometimes (c) rarely

21. Have you ever thought of leaving your partner because of unresolved conflicts?
    (a) never (b) sometimes (c) frequently

22. When alone together, do you frequently get on each other's nerves?
    (a) rarely (b) occasionally (c) frequently

23. Do you ever worry about how long your marriage will last?
    (a) rarely (b) occasionally (c) frequently

24. Do you and your spouse do a lot of things together?
    (a) frequently (b) occasionally (c) rarely

25. Are you and your spouse openly affectionate with each other?
    (a) frequently (b) occasionally (c) rarely

QUIZ 30

How Can Career Conflicts Lead to Marriage Chaos?

1. Do you get more satisfaction out of your job than you do out of your home life?
   (a) never (b) sometimes (c) frequently

2. If you receive a lot of praise at work, would you be able to share your good feelings with your family?
   (a) yes (b) maybe (c) no

3. Do you feel you're not doing enough to help your spouse cope with the financial burden of the family?
   (a) no (b) maybe (c) yes

4. Do you feel it's important to belong to the right clubs in order to help your spouse get ahead at work?
   (a) maybe (b) sometimes (c) yes

5. Do you feel there's little hope of changing careers right now, because of your family situation?
   (a) rarely (b) sometimes (c) often

6. Would you spend a lot of time away from the family, taking courses to get ahead in your job?
   (a) would consider it (b) would not consider it (c) would definitely consider it

7. Would you take a permanent job that had a long commute?
(a) no (b) maybe (c) yes

8. Is your spouse satisfied with your career choice?
(a) yes (b) maybe (c) no

9. Do you feel your spouse uses the job as an excuse to spend less time at home?
(a) no (b) maybe (c) yes

10. Does it feel like you and your spouse spend too much time working, with little time left for each other?
(a) rarely (b) occasionally (c) frequently

11. Does having the responsibility of a family give you a clearer focus of your future career goals?
(a) yes (b) maybe (c) no

12. Do you admire your spouse's ambition?
(a) yes (b) maybe (c) no

13. Do you wish your spouse were more ambitious?
(a) rarely (b) sometimes (c) often

14. Have you had trouble keeping jobs in the past?
(a) no (b) occasionally (c) yes

15. Do you think your marriage would run a lot smoother if your spouse were involved in a different job?
(a) no (b) maybe (c) yes

16. Would you be very disappointed if you didn't achieve your career goals?
(a) a little (b) somewhat (c) a lot

17. Do you feel you're doing the best you can to provide for your family's needs?
(a) yes (b) maybe (c) no

18. Have you been able to get ahead in your career because of your spouse's help?
(a) yes (b) maybe (c) no

19. Are money worries on your mind a lot?
(a) no (b) sometimes (c) yes

20. If you got a bonus at work, would you buy something nice for your spouse?
(a) yes (b) maybe (c) no

21. If you got a bonus at work, do you feel you should keep most of it?
(a) no (b) maybe (c) yes

22. If your spouse was unhappy with your current job, would you consider a change just to keep peace in the family?
(a) probably (b) maybe (c) no

23. Do you feel marriage has sidetracked you from your original career goals?
 (a) no (b) maybe (c) yes

24. In your current job, do you feel there's no one better than you at what you do?
 (a) yes (b) maybe (c) no

25. Are you willing to stay late at work, even when it's not really necessary?
 (a) rarely (b) sometimes (c) always

26. Do you volunteer to stay late at the job?
 (a) sometimes (b) frequently (c) usually

27. If one of the kids gets sick, and both you and your spouse work, do you take turns staying home?
 (a) usually (b) sometimes (c) rarely

28. Do you get upset when you have to spend time by yourself because of your spouse's erratic work schedule?
 (a) sometimes (b) usually (c) always

29. If you both come back from a grueling day at work, who would make dinner for the family?
 (a) whoever got home first (b) both (c) wife

30. Would you turn down a well-paying job if it caused conflict within the family?
 (a) probably (b) possibly (c) no

QUIZ 31

Is Your Home Life Sabotaging Your Marriage?

1. Even though you couldn't afford it, would you insist on living in a particular neighborhood because of the status?
 (a) no (b) depends (c) yes

2. Do you feel a home in the suburbs is important because it's the only place to bring up children?
 (a) no (b) maybe (c) yes

3. Does it make you uncomfortable when things get out of place around the house?
 (a) rarely (b) occasionally (c) frequently

4. Would you be willing to make any sacrifice to keep your family in a nice home?
 (a) depends (b) no (c) yes

5. Does your mate feel you spend more than you should on new appliances and furnishings for the house?
 (a) rarely (b) occasionally (c) frequently

6. Do you spend so much time working around your house at nights and on weekends that you have little energy left for your family?
   (a) rarely (b) occasionally (c) frequently

7. Even though you have the time and energy, do you find your house never seems to get clean?
   (a) rarely (b) occasionally (c) frequently

8. Do you find that even though you're proud of your house and want it to look its best, you never seem to have the time to do the minor repairs necessary to keep it up?
   (a) rarely (b) occasionally (c) frequently

9. Do you feel comfortable if your spouse's friends visit your home unexpectedly?
   (a) yes (b) usually (c) no

10. Does your spouse object to your spending money on the house, even though it's often for necessities?
    (a) no (b) usually (c) yes

11. Do you enjoy having a lot of mechanical gadgets around the house?
    (a) no (b) some (c) yes

12. Do you have a whole assortment of household equipment in the basement that somehow never seems to get used?
    (a) no (b) maybe (c) yes

13. Are you only happy living in a certain type of house and in a certain type of neighborhood?
    (a) no (b) somewhat (c) yes

14. Did you and your spouse agree on the type of home furnishings you have?
    (a) yes (b) mainly (c) no

15. Would you rather buy new furniture than go on a vacation?
    (a) depends (b) sometimes (c) usually

QUIZ 32

Is Your Marriage Getting Enough R&R?

1. Is it difficult for you and your spouse to plan a vacation because you have different amusement interests?
   (a) never (b) usually (c) always

2. Do you often take separate vacations?
   (a) rarely (b) sometimes (c) frequently

3. Could you even enjoy a family vacation involving the children and in-laws?
   (a) sometimes (b) maybe (c) never

4. Do you find you argue more when on vacation?
   (a) sometimes (b) occasionally (c) usually

5. Do you think a vacation is a good excuse for you to walk around looking like a slob?
   (a) no (b) maybe (c) yes

6. Is it difficult for you and your spouse to spend a lot of time together without getting on each other's nerves?
   (a) no (b) maybe (c) yes

7. When having dinner out with your spouse, do you often run out of things to talk about?
   (a) no (b) seldom (c) often

8. Can you find something humorous in an emotionally charged situation?
   (a) usually (b) sometimes (c) rarely

9. Do you and your mate share a lot of activities together?
   (a) yes (b) some (c) no

10. When invited to a social function, do you look forward to having a good time with your mate?
    (a) yes (b) maybe (c) no

11. Do you and your mate try to get away together even if it's only for a few days, so you both can be alone?
    (a) yes (b) sometimes (c) no

12. Do you get uncomfortable when going to a party with your mate, fearing that you will be embarrassed?
    (a) no (b) sometimes (c) yes

13. Do you and your family make a regular habit of socializing together?
    (a) yes (b) sometimes (c) no

14. Do you and your mate quarrel over your choice of friends?
    (a) no (b) sometimes (c) yes

15. Without having to think about it, could you name three things you and your mate enjoy doing together?
    (a) yes (b) with difficulty (c) no

16. Do you reminisce about the funny things that family members have done in the past?
    (a) often (b) sometimes (c) rarely

17. Does a day spent with your spouse make life's difficulties easier to bear?
    (a) frequently (b) occasionally (c) rarely

18. Does your family enjoy telling jokes and funny stories to one another?
    (a) often (b) sometimes (c) rarely

19. Do you and your spouse do things together without the children?
    (a) yes (b) maybe (c) no

20. Do you use humor to put down other family members?
    (a) rarely (b) sometimes (c) frequently

21. When the family's under a lot of stress, are there some activities you like to do to diffuse the tension?
    (a) yes (b) some (c) no

22. Should you laugh at a child's innocent mistakes, clumsiness or lack of coordination?
    (a) no (b) rarely (c) yes

23. Would you use humor to try to cheer up a moody child?
    (a) yes (b) maybe (c) no

24. Do you agree that a family with a good sense of humor has a better chance of staying together?
    (a) yes (b) maybe (c) no

25. Did you enjoy taking trips with your family when you were a child?
    (a) yes (b) rarely (c) no

QUIZ 33

Do You and Your Spouse Feel the Same About Love?

1. Do you feel special just knowing that your spouse is in love with you?
   (a) yes (b) usually (c) no

2. Do you credit your spouse with being responsible for the success and happiness you've had in life since being married?
   (a) a lot (b) some (c) none

3. Do you feel that you love your spouse more than the other way around?
   (a) rarely (b) sometimes (c) often

4. Do you consider yourself to be a very affectionate person?
   (a) usually (b) sometimes (c) rarely

5. Is your love for your partner the same as when you were first married?
   (a) more (b) same (c) less

6. Do you feel that married love helps a person feel more fulfilled as a man or woman?
   (a) yes (b) usually (c) no

7. Do you and your spouse still experiment with new ways to make love?
   (a) yes (b) sometimes (c) rarely

8. Do your fantasies while making love include your spouse?
   (a) yes (b) sometimes (c) no

9. Is it difficult for you to show your spouse how much you really care?
   (a) no (b) rarely (c) yes

10. Do you sometimes fear your spouse has lost interest in you?
   (a) no (b) rarely (c) yes

11. Is your marriage relationship more satisfying than any other area of your life?
   (a) yes (b) usually (c) no

12. Do you tell your spouse everything?
   (a) depends (b) no (c) yes

13. Do you often wish you were still single?
   (a) no (b) rarely (c) yes

14. Do you think it's important to keep a little mystery about yourself and your experiences from your mate by holding back some information?
   (a) no (b) rarely (c) yes

15. Do you think each new stage of your marriage is going to get better, so that you look forward to it with happy anticipation?
   (a) often (b) sometimes (c) seldom

16. When you look at your spouse's naked body, does it still appeal to you?
   (a) usually (b) sometimes (c) rarely

17. Do you feel you've gotten to know your spouse so well that you can almost predict the behavior in any given situation?
   (a) often (b) sometimes (c) rarely

18. Do you often look at your spouse and wonder what happened to the person you married?
   (a) no (b) rarely (c) yes

19. Can you and your spouse agree about religious matters?
   (a) usually (b) sometimes (c) rarely

20. Does your mate tell you that he/she is in love with you?
   (a) often (b) sometimes (c) rarely

21. How often do you tell your mate?
   (a) frequently (b) occasionally (c) rarely

22. Whenever you think of your spouse, do you feel you made the right choice?
   (a) yes (b) usually (c) no

23. Do you find it's not as exciting to make love to your spouse as it once was?
   (a) rarely (b) sometimes (c) usually

24. Do you feel your spouse's style of lovemaking has changed?
   (a) no (b) maybe (c) yes

25. Do you wish that it would change?
    (a) seldom (b) sometimes (c) usually

26. Were you and your spouse more experimental in your lovemaking in the beginning of your marriage than you are now?
    (a) a little (b) some (c) a lot

27. Do you occasionally find yourself getting bored with your spouse's style of lovemaking?
    (a) rarely (b) sometimes (c) often

28. Have you ever thought of leaving your mate for any reason?
    (a) rarely (b) sometimes (c) often

29. Have your feelings about your partner changed since you've been married?
    (a) no (b) some (c) yes

30. Have you grown to understand each other more?
    (a) yes (b) some (c) no

31. Do you think you've grown apart from each other since being married?
    (a) no (b) some (c) yes

32. Do you think so far your marriage has been a successful maturation process for the both of you?
    (a) yes (b) mostly (c) no

33. Has your spouse fulfilled all your needs, both sexual and personal, as you had hoped?
    (a) mostly (b) some (c) very few

34. Were you attracted to your spouse because he/she seemed like the sort of person you like?
    (a) yes (b) maybe (c) no

35. Are you convinced that you want to share the rest of your life with your spouse?
    (a) yes (b) maybe (c) not totally

QUIZ 34

How Well Do You and Your Mate Communicate?

1. You're in the kitchen cooking your dinner when your spouse walks in the door, late as usual. Feeling as steamed as some of the vegetables, do you turn and:
   (a) tell your mate that being late is unfortunate, and as a result the food may be a little overcooked
   (b) vow that from now on it's going to be peanut butter and jelly
   (c) accuse your mate of always being thoughtlessly late

2. You notice that your spouse has forgotten to replace the toothpaste cap again. Would you march downstairs and:
   (a) politely ask for more consideration when it comes to these little things

(b) accuse your mate of being a slob
(c) get your revenge by hanging wet underwear all over the bathroom

3. You and your spouse are looking at new cars. While discussing the pros and cons about mileage, insurance, etc., do you also tell the salesman:
   (a) about your spouse's good driving record
   (b) that your spouse would be better off driving a tank but probably couldn't park that in the garage either
   (c) that your spouse is the featured star of the accident-of-the-month club

4. There's something bugging you and you can't wait to get it off your chest. Do you tell your spouse you want to discuss it:
   (a) at a time that's mutually good for both of you
   (b) just before going to bed at night
   (c) just before rushing off to work in the morning

5. When you feel like arguing, do you think the best place to do it is:
   (a) while sitting down somewhere comfortable and facing one another
   (b) anywhere you can stand and tower over your mate
   (c) in the car

6. It's your birthday and your spouse has bought you a present. It's a stuffed fish with a clock in its stomach, which you hate. Do you urge your mate to:
   (a) take it back but make some kind of excuse not to hurt the person's feelings
   (b) put it on the mantel at once and tell yourself that it's the thought that counts
   (c) give up the charge card because this purchase shows that he/she can't make a rational decision

7. You're at a housewarming party and your host tells you that he just got a new water bed. Then he winks wickedly and asks if you and your mate would like to try it. Would you chuckle and say:
   (a) no thanks, maybe later on
   (b) me...on a water bed with my spouse...even the thought makes me seasick
   (c) oh, we already have one of our own

8. You're involved in a discussion with your spouse about your favorite subject, foreign films. Knowing your mate doesn't really like or understand them, should you:
   (a) offer to drop the subject and move on to something else
   (b) listen politely and try to educate your spouse to your point of view
   (c) tell your mate that his/her opinion is worth bunk

9. You like your mate to call you at least once a day to talk about your plans for the evening. But your mate often forgets. Do you:
   (a) forget about it, but try to find out the reason why
   (b) angrily call and remind your spouse
   (c) nag

10. You and your spouse are at a party and you both know what an outrageous but harmless flirt your neighbor is. You start to sizzle when you see your spouse asked into the kitchen for the fifth time on some flimsy excuse. Do you:
    (a) decide to be a good sport and laugh it off
    (b) go into the kitchen for a glass of water
    (c) decide to lose five pounds and pay more attention to your mate from now on

QUIZ 35

Does Your Mate Also Rate as Your Best Friend?

1. Does your spouse spend a lot of time involved in outside hobbies with other people?
   (a) no (b) maybe (c) yes

2. Are you equally involved in your own personal pursuits?
   (a) yes (b) maybe (c) no

3. Do you sometimes feel lonely?
   (a) rarely (b) occasionally (c) frequently

4. Even though you can't do everything with your spouse, is it enough to know he/she loves you?
   (a) yes (b) usually (c) no

5. Is your spouse always available when needed?
   (a) yes (b) often (c) no

6. Can you and your spouse spend a lot of time together without getting on each other's nerves?
   (a) usually (b) sometimes (c) rarely

7. Do you and your spouse try to spend as much time together as you can?
   (a) yes (b) maybe (c) no

8. Can you and your spouse spend time apart from each other without it causing a problem in your relationship?
   (a) yes (b) maybe (c) no

9. Do you encourage your spouse to do things without you which he/she likes to do?
   (a) yes (b) maybe (c) no

10. Would you feel rejected if your spouse did a lot of things without you?
    (a) no (b) maybe (c) yes

11. Do you often feel guilty that you don't have enough time to spend with your spouse?
    (a) no (b) sometimes (c) yes

12. Do you often wish you and your mate were more compatible in your interests and activities?
    (a) no (b) sometimes (c) yes

13. Do you spend so much time at work or work-related activities that you have very little time left for your spouse?
    (a) no (b) sometimes (c) yes

14. Do you have to nag your spouse to spend more time at home with you?
    (a) no (b) depends (c) yes

15. Would you go to a company party alone, if for some reason your spouse couldn't go with you?
    (a) yes (b) depends (c) no

16. When your spouse is not around, do you find it very easy to keep yourself occupied with things to do?
    (a) usually (b) sometimes (c) rarely

17. Do you panic at the thought of being separated from your spouse even for short periods of time?
    (a) no (b) sometimes (c) yes

18. Do you and your spouse ever talk about anything besides the family and children?
    (a) yes (b) sometimes (c) no

19. Did you have a good time with your spouse the last time you both went out socially?
    (a) yes (b) maybe (c) no

20. Do you and your spouse try to make a regular habit of going out alone together, to take a break from the family?
    (a) yes (b) depends (c) no

21. Do you feel that often it's the little things you do together, like taking a walk in the woods, that brings you closer together?
    (a) yes (b) usually (c) no

22. Does your spouse like your friends?
    (a) yes (b) some (c) no

23. Do you like your spouse's friends?
    (a) yes (b) some (c) no

24. Do you ever get jealous of your spouse doing something without you?
    (a) rarely (b) frequently (c) usually

25. Do you expect your spouse to pick your social entertainment and choose your friends?
    (a) no (b) maybe (c) yes

QUIZ 36

Are You and Your Spouse as Close as You'd Like to Be?

1. If you had a serious problem, would it be easy for you to confide in your spouse?
   (a) yes (b) depends (c) no

2. Is it easy for you to reveal your most intimate thoughts and feelings to your spouse?
   (a) yes (b) usually (c) no

3. Do you enjoy yourself more if your spouse is also involved in the activity?
   (a) yes (b) mostly (c) no

4. Does your greatest satisfaction in life come from your home and family?
   (a) yes (b) mostly (c) no

5. Does your greatest satisfaction in life come from your job or career?
   (a) no (b) somewhat (c) yes

6. Do you get upset when you can't control certain events in your life?
   (a) sometimes (b) rarely (c) a lot

7. Do you get upset if your spouse doesn't spend most of his/her available time with you?
   (a) no (b) sometimes (c) yes

8. Do you feel that a lot of your happiness in life depends on your spouse?
   (a) yes (b) maybe (c) no

9. Do you think that being in love makes a person vulnerable?
   (a) no (b) sometimes (c) yes

10. If you had to rate your partner right now, would you say his/her most important quality is compatibility?
    (a) yes (b) maybe (c) no

11. Even though married, do you still value your individuality?
    (a) yes (b) usually (c) no

12. Is the reassurance that you'll be cared for by your spouse very important to you?
    (a) yes (b) maybe (c) no

13. Did you come from a family that was outwardly affectionate?
    (a) yes (b) somewhat (c) no

14. Would you rather be involved with your spouse in doing something even if the activity was not one you excelled at?
    (a) yes (b) sometimes (c) no

15. Have you ever been able to live alone for long periods of time without minding it?
    (a) no (b) seldom (c) yes

16. Do you put a lot of effort into your marriage because it's the most important relationship in your life?
    (a) yes (b) maybe (c) no

17. Would you be upset if you found out that your spouse was keeping secrets from you?
    (a) yes (b) depends (c) no

18. Would you be upset if you caught your spouse in a lie?
    (a) yes (b) usually (c) no

19. Do you do little things, like sending flowers, sending a card or making a phone call, to show your spouse how much you care?
    (a) yes (b) often (c) no

20. Do you feel any kind of affectionate behavior, i.e., kissing, touching, etc., should be reserved strictly for the bedroom?
    (a) no (b) depends (c) yes

21. Are you playful and openly affectionate with your children?
    (a) yes (b) does not apply (c) no

22. Do you get upset when your child hugs you?
    (a) no (b) does not apply (c) yes

23. Can you easily talk about your feelings?
    (a) yes (b) usually (c) no

24. Has your spouse ever seen you cry?
    (a) yes (b) sometimes (c) no

25. Has it become easier for you to express your feelings since you've gotten married?
    (a) a lot (b) somewhat (c) no

To Be Answered by Wives Only

QUIZ 37

Can a Marriage Survive Sexual Hang-Ups?

1. Do you suffer from painful intercourse?
   (a) rarely (b) sometimes (c) often

2. Do you feel you're as good in bed as your spouse would like you to be?
   (a) yes (b) usually (c) no

3. Do you often get uncomfortable when naked in front of your spouse, because your body isn't as attractive as you'd like it to be?
   (a) no (b) sometimes (c) yes

4. Does it embarrass you that your breasts are too large (too small)?
   (a) no (b) at times (c) yes

5. Can you tell your husband what turns you on in bed?
   (a) yes (b) usually (c) no

6. Do you prefer certain sex practices compared to others?
   (a) a few (b) some (c) a lot

7. Would you refuse to try a new sexual technique or position, even though your spouse really wanted to?
   (a) no (b) depends (c) yes

8. Do you frequently achieve orgasm?
   (a) frequently (b) occasionally (c) rarely

9. Would you consider using a device for sexual stimulation during love-making?
   (a) maybe (b) no (c) yes

10. Would you be upset if your partner wanted to change your usual routine of lovemaking, i.e., the place or the time of day?
    (a) no (b) unlikely (c) yes

11. Would you be embarrassed if someone told you a dirty joke at a party?
    (a) no (b) depends (c) yes

12. Do you feel that masturbation is an unpleasant act?
    (a) no (b) depends (c) yes

13. Do you feel ridiculous wearing the sexy lingerie your husband bought you for your birthday?
    (a) no (b) depends (c) yes

14. Can you undress in front of your husband?
    (a) yes (b) depends (c) no

15. Is sex an important part of your relationship with your spouse?
    (a) yes (b) depends (c) no

To Be Answered by Husbands Only

QUIZ 38

Can a Marriage Survive Sexual Hang-Ups?

1. Do you ever get anxious about the quality of your sexual performance?
   (a) rarely (b) occasionally (c) frequently

2. Do you appreciate it when your mate compliments you on your sexual performance?
   (a) yes (b) sometimes (c) no

3. Do you think a lot of your masculinity depends on your sexual performance?
   (a) no (b) depends (c) yes

4. Have you ever been impotent?
   (a) rarely (b) occasionally (c) frequently

5. Is your wife very understanding and supportive when this happens?
   (a) yes (b) sometimes (c) no

6. Have you ever had any trouble with premature ejaculation?
   (a) rarely (b) occasionally (c) frequently

7. Is your partner willing to work with you to solve this problem?
   (a) frequently (b) occasionally (c) rarely

8. Have you ever fantasized about making love with another woman?
   (a) rarely (b) occasionally (c) frequently

9. Do you fear that as you get older, you won't be able to perform as well as you do now?
   (a) rarely (b) occasionally (c) frequently

10. Are you willing to experiment with sex by trying new times, new places and different positions?
    (a) yes (b) sometimes (c) no

11. Do you feel inadequate if your partner does not have an orgasm?
    (a) sometimes (b) often (c) yes

12. Do you like to tell your spouse how she turns you on in very explicit sexual terms?
    (a) yes (b) rarely (c) no

13. Do you get concerned that your partner will reject you because you can't perform sexually?
    (a) rarely (b) occasionally (c) frequently

14. Instead of finding ways to reinvigorate your own waning sexual feelings, do you blame your sexual blahs on your spouse?
    (a) rarely (b) occasionally (c) frequently

15. Do you feel more comfortable discussing your sexual preferences with your buddies than with your wife?
    (a) no (b) depends (c) yes

QUIZ 39

Is Stress Hurting Your Marriage?

1. Have you suddenly started coming home from work a lot later than usual?
   (a) no (b) maybe (c) yes

2. Have you suddenly changed your manner of dressing, i.e., going from conservative to flamboyant, or vice versa?
   (a) no (b) maybe (c) yes

3. Have you suddenly started talking about buying something big and expensive that you can hardly afford?
   (a) a little (b) some (c) a lot

4. Have you noticed that you've begun to gain or lose a lot of weight lately?
   (a) no (b) some (c) yes

5. Have you begun to take any kind of medication to calm you down?
   (a) no (b) some (c) yes

6. Have you started to bring home a lot of work from the office?
   (a) no (b) more often (c) yes

7. Is there a place set aside at home where you can go and just relax for a few minutes?
   (a) yes (b) depends (c) no

8. Do you find that you're more tired than you used to be?
   (a) seldom (b) somewhat (c) more often

9. Have you suddenly stopped doing things that you used to enjoy very much?
   (a) no (b) somewhat (c) yes

10. Has your sexual performance diminished?
    (a) no (b) maybe (c) yes

11. Are your moods more unpredictable than usual?
    (a) no (b) maybe (c) yes

12. Do you feel you can depend on your spouse for moral support?
    (a) a lot (b) somewhat (c) doubtful

13. Are you more active in community involvement?
    (a) about the same (b) some more (c) a lot more

14. If you've just been rejected on a job or insulted by a friend, do you think you would recover your spirits in a few days?
    (a) yes (b) depends (c) no

15. Do you want to be left alone more than usual?
    (a) no (b) depends (c) yes

16. Have you been having trouble sleeping?
    (a) no (b) depends (c) yes

17. Have you become concerned about the strange thoughts that seem to be shooting through your mind?
    (a) no (b) depends (c) yes

18. Have you always had some very important goals in life that you've just suddenly given up?
    (a) no (b) depends (c) yes

19. Has your partner mentioned noticing a big change in your attitude or behavior lately?
    (a) no (b) depends (c) yes

20. Are you generally eager to get out of bed in the morning?
    (a) yes (b) depends (c) no

Scoring Instructions for Part Three

Rating

The eighteen quizzes in Part Three are designed to:

1) Give you new insights into yourself and your mate.
2) Point out your marriage trouble spots.
3) Show you how your marriage is functioning overall.

Scoring

To change your answers into a point value, use the following scoring systems:

1) For each (a) answer—give yourself 3 points.
2) For each (b) answer—give yourself 2 points.
3) For each (c) answer—give yourself 1 point.

Add up the total number of points for each quiz.

Note: use this scoring key for Quizzes 22 through 39.

Evaluating

Beginning with Quiz 22, find the range which fits your score, and read the corresponding explanation. If you and your spouse have taken the quizzes together, this is where the two of you can finally compare notes on the similarities and differences in your individual answers to specific quizzes, as well as your overall scores.

QUIZ 22
How Does Sex Rate in Your Marriage?

One of the basic advantages of marriage is sexual fulfillment. For some people, this ongoing, enduring relationship is an important criteria for partner selection. For others the opposite is true. They can only feel comfortable with one-night stands. How do you feel about sex in your marriage?

If you scored between:
61–75 You get a great deal of satisfaction from knowing that you have a permanent sexual partner, who is available to you no matter what. Your relationship makes you feel very relaxed and content. And you thrive on the intimacy that results from sharing yourself with a mate.
43–60 You like the sexual freedom that marriage provides. And you like the security of knowing that your partner is indeed yours. Occasionally you feel bored by the restraints of having to be loyal to one person. But overall, you would be unhappy in any other kind of living situation.
25–42 The sexual freedom of marriage makes you feel uncomfortable because it is difficult for you to share yourself completely with another person. You need to feel more trusting of your partner. And this trust can develop the longer your marriage endures.

QUIZ 23
What Are the Sexual Trouble Spots in Your Marriage?

Since sex can be one of the main aspects in marriage, a couple can become very unhappy when things go wrong in this area.

If you scored between:
83–105 You have no problems with sex in your marriage. You're quite satisfied with your mate. And you're both able to cope with whatever difficulties may come up that might strain the relationship.
59–82 Even though there are pressures on your relationship, you and your

spouse are able to make a reasonably healthy adjustment.

35–58 There are many pressures in your marriage that you and your mate have not been able to resolve. As a result, the marital bond between you and your partner is weakening.

QUIZ 24
Do You And Your Mate Operate on the Same Wavelength?

In marriage, the energy levels and sexual appetites of a couple may not mesh for one reason or another. This can become a problem when neither partner takes the time to understand and appreciate the other's needs.

If you scored between:

96–120 You're a high-tempo person with a lot of energy to burn. You're interested in everything that goes on around you and have very few problems adjusting to new and different things in your life.

68–95 You're a middle-of-the-roader in your interests and expectations. You could blend well with either a high-tempo personality or be equally happy with a low-tempo type. Your well-balanced nature is one of your virtues.

40–67 There aren't too many things that you can or want to do. It's not easy for you to adapt to new situations. And if you were matched with a high-tempo personality, the two of you would be miserable together, unless each made an effort to understand and accept the differences.

QUIZ 25
Do You Have a Healthy Marriage?

A healthy marriage depends on many things, e.g., how you meet each other's needs, whether you support and encourage each other, how well you each communicate, how much freedom you each have to do your own thing and whether marriage has lived up to your prior expectations.

If you scored between:

61–75 Your marriage has passed its test with flying colors.

43–60 Your marriage is doing all right, despite a few troubling symptoms that may need watching in the future.

25–42 Right now, your marriage needs work, but you've taken the first step to recovery with a dose of reality from this quiz.

QUIZ 26
What Do Wives Expect Out of Marriage?

In today's marriages, some women believe it doesn't matter who cooks dinner, who diapers the baby, or who works outside the home to put food on the table. Others however, disagree. What type of wife are you?

If you scored between:

61–75 You're a traditionalist through and through. There's nothing you enjoy better than tending to home and hearth while your husband sits, with pipe and slippers, reading the financial pages.

43–60 You like a relationship where the duties and responsibilities are shared to a degree. But the majority of household chores and errands are still your domain.

25–42 You're very independent, even though married. The only way your house is going to run smoothly is if everybody pitches in and does their share.

QUIZ 27
What Do Husbands Expect Out of Marriage?

Some husbands would only be happy with an old-fashioned wife. Others are quite content to share the household duties with their spouses.

If you scored between:

61–75 You want a wife who's going to cater to the home and family's needs first and foremost.

43–60 You don't mind helping out with what you consider wifely chores once in a while. Even if your wife worked, you would feel she was also responsible for the home.

25–42 You believe whoever gets home first should cook dinner. And whoever passes the store should pick up the groceries. You don't believe that gender dictates duties around the house.

QUIZ 28
Is Financial Stress Hurting Your Family?

Not having enough money can put a lot of stress on a marital relationship. Some couples find successful ways to cope. Others are driven apart.

If you scored between:

83–105 The way you spend or earn money does not affect the security of your marriage.

59–82 Some of your marriage problems are directly related to the way you handle money. A more careful approach to budgeting could be a solution.

35–58 Many of the stresses in your marriage are caused by the way you handle or think about money.

QUIZ 29
How Satisfying Is Your Marriage?

Do you and your partner do all you can to make each other happy and to fulfill each other's needs?

If you scored between:

61–75 The answer is a definite "yes."

43–60 Marriage succeeds in satisfying your needs most of the time.

25–42 You often ask yourself why you ever married, because it hasn't turned out the way you expected.

QUIZ 30
How Can Career Conflicts Lead to Marriage Chaos?

Juggling a career and a family isn't easy. And many times this places an additional strain on the marriage. How is yours working out?

If you scored between:

76–90 Your marriage is doing well despite the demands your job makes on your time and family.

51–75 Sometimes it seems almost impossible, and you don't know where you get the strength, but you're still able to balance your career and your home life without too many difficulties.

30–50 Many times you feel you have to decide between your job and your family. And it's difficult for you to understand where your priorities really lie.

QUIZ 31
Is Your Home Life Sabotaging Your Marriage?

More than a shelter for married people, a home is a physical, financial and psychological investment. And it can become the center of marital stress.

If you scored between:

35–45 Your home is a safe, satisfying haven for yourself and your family.

25–34 You sometimes let your personal problems influence the way you treat your home, i.e., cleanliness, disorder, etc.

15–24 You may be experiencing a lot of stress in your marriage because of unreasonable expectations about your home, i.e., cleanliness, disorder, living in a certain neighborhood, etc.

QUIZ 32
Is Your Marriage Getting Enough R&R?

It's true. The family that plays together, stays together.

If you scored between:

61–75 It may seem like fun and games, but the light moments your family spends together are helping it thrive.

43–60 You're already doing some things with your family. Why not try a little harder. The results will be worth it.

25–42 There's nothing wrong with pursuing your own interests, but you should also find ways to have fun with your family as a group.

QUIZ 33
Do You And Your Spouse Feel the Same About Love?

People marry for love. And the most obvious sign that a marriage is in trouble is when you feel love is missing from your relationship.

If you scored between:
83–105 Your relationship is strong and satisfying. Even though there are times when you doubt and even dislike your spouse, you're still deeply in love.
59–82 When you think of your spouse, you feel warm, positive feelings that should assure you that your relationship is in good health.
35–58 You feel there is a missing ingredient in your marriage compared to the way it used to be. But you might be able to get your marriage back on track if you take the time to find out why this is so.

QUIZ 34
How Well Do You and Your Mate Communicate?

No matter what your marriage style, the secret to success is the same for all—good communication.

If you scored between:
16–30 You are a good communicator. You are open about your feelings and can speak your mind without being abrasive.
10–15 You tend to use communication to manipulate others. And if you want to help your marriage, you should try to be a little more understanding and open about your feelings.

QUIZ 35
Does Your Mate Also Rate as Your Best Friend?

It's all right to do your own thing. But the farther apart you and your spouse grow in sharing common interests, the more stress you're likely to feel in your marriage.

If you scored between:
61–75 Your companionship is one of the strongest satisfactions in your marriage.
43–60 You like to go your own way, but you still share many activities with your spouse and family.
25–42 You choose to spend more time away from your spouse than you spend together. Perhaps this is a good time to ask yourself why.

QUIZ 36
Are You and Your Spouse as Close as You'd Like to Be?

Your marriage can be as intimate as you want to make it or as distant as two strangers. Either arrangement is fine, providing it's mutually satisfying to both people. But very often one spouse may be totally unaware of the other's needs.

If you scored between:
61–75 You're very satisfied with your relationship and feel that it is living up to your needs and expectations.
43–60 Although you would like your spouse to be closer to you, you feel that your relationship is sufficiently close.
25–42 Although married, you often feel lonely because an emotional flow is lacking in your relationship.

QUIZZES 37 & 38
Can a Marriage Survive Sexual Hang-Ups?

People often enter marriage with tremendous differences in their sexual needs, preferences as well as a host of cultural and familial taboos. As a result, sexual satisfaction can become a problem for one or both partners unless you're willing to discuss it and find a mutual solution. (Use the following scoring system for each quiz.)

If you scored between:

35–45 In relation to sex, you're willing to try anything.

25–34 There are some sexual preferences you and your spouse do not share. But overall you have a satisfactory relationship.

15–24 You have very rigid ideas about sex. But if you try to become aware that your way is not the only one right way, you may learn to accept your partner's needs for pleasure as well.

QUIZ 39
Is Stress Hurting Your Marriage?

When one partner in a marriage is going through a difficult time, it places stress on the marriage, which can have either positive or negative effects on the relationship.

If you scored between:

50–60 You've already been through a lot of problems with your spouse. But no matter how difficult they've been, the experience has brought you closer together.

36–49 When those daily stresses start your marriage spinning off course, your relationship is strong enough to fight back.

20–35 You tend to fall apart in stressful situations. As a result, you often react with impatience rather than sympathy when your spouse has a problem. If you don't eventually learn how to cope, this behavior could put your relationship in jeopardy.

Conclusion:

What's the Key to Marital Happiness?

MARRIAGE in the eighties and beyond is going to be more exciting than ever, with less rules and more options. And if you want to have a satisfying relationship, you'd better be prepared to toss out the old formulas and chart your own course.

Although some of your decisions have been predetermined in childhood, where you formulated certain ideals about a dream partner, wanting to marry for love alone is not enough to keep a couple together in today's hectic world.

The best way to insure happiness is to first know yourself in order to find a deeper commitment to and stronger compatibility with another person. That's how *Test Your Marriage I.Q.* can continue to help. It is a tool.

Whether you are single and still searching for the perfect mate, or already married, the personal profile which you've just constructed with the quizzes in this book can help to keep you afloat in today's matrimonial seas.

Are you ready for marriage?

If you've taken the quizzes and scored well in Parts One and Two, you've probably found that you're a very people-oriented person with a great potential for marriage. And as long as you're careful in selecting someone who shares many of your personal needs, ideals and characteristics, you can take a deep breath, relax and look forward to wedded bliss.

On the other hand, don't be disappointed if some of your scores are low. These scores point to the areas which might require constructive action on your part and hopefully make some necessary and positive changes for the future.

Is marriage right for you?

If, when taking the quizzes, you've discovered that you're somewhere out in marital left field, be thankful that you found out when you did and don't let your parents or friends push you down that middle aisle. You just might need some more time to evaluate your needs and expectations. And remember: Everybody isn't meant for marriage.

Is your marriage everything you'd like it to be?

Far from being the end of a goal, as many couples think, marriage is only the beginning. As a matter of fact, few married couples ever achieve their *full* potential for happiness. So remember: It's never too late.

And no matter how satisfied you think you are with your mate, you can always use the information and insights gleaned from the quizzes to build a much stronger relationship. This is particularly important in today's marriages where so many couples are balancing two careers and sharing a variety of household roles.

If you and your partner don't share the attitude that marriage is a two-way street, if you're not willing to accept the day-to-day discomforts for better or for worse, and if you're not going to pull together—forsaking all others—your relationship might be on shaky ground.

Marriage, because of its presumable security, permanence and sexual exclusivity, is still the way for most people to achieve a happy and fulfilling relationship. That's not to say that bad marriages don't exist. But the problems are most probably with the individuals, not the institution.

There's no magic formula that can guarantee marital happiness for every couple. But if you've taken the quizzes with your spouse or potential spouse you are closer to having your own personalized plan for marital success. The rest is up to you.

NOTE: This book has given you the best information the authors could possibly provide. And while we hope that the readers will be grateful for the useful and informative comments contained herein, we don't encourage anyone to make an important life decision based solely on the facts put forth in this book.

Twenty-Five Common Marriage Myths

1. Having an affair can help a faltering marriage.
2. It's easy to change your spouse once you're married.
3. It's possible to expect another person to fulfill all your needs.
4. If you can make it through the first five years, you don't have anything to worry about.
5. People who marry a second time always learn from their first mistakes.
6. An expression of jealousy is a sure sign of love.
7. If you only had enough money, the marriage would never have any problems.
8. You can live on love.
9. Children will always hold a marriage together.
10. You can't help getting to know a person if you live with him/her long enough.
11. If the sex is good, that's all you need to keep a marriage together.
12. If your partner wants sex more than you do, he/she is the one who's being unreasonable.
13. There are correct and incorrect ways of having sex.
14. After two people have been together for a while, it's common to lose sexual interest in each other.
15. A husband who helps out at home is henpecked.
16. A wife who works has a husband who is too inadequate to support her.
17. When two people never argue, that's a sign of a happy marriage.
18. To be happily married, you must always give in to your spouse.
19. The husband should always be in charge of the finances.
20. It's important to keep a marriage together for the sake of the children.
21. The reason why my marriage isn't happy is that my husband/wife doesn't understand me.
22. When making love, there is only one good position.
23. Using pornographic books or movies for sexual stimulation in marriage is harmful.
24. Using a chemical substance will make sex feel great.
25. All your marriage problems can be solved in the bedroom.

Useful and Interesting Marriage Statistics

Would you believe that:

1. Ninety-seven percent of all individuals marry.
2. Four out of five individuals will remarry.
3. Eighty percent of all teenage marriages will end in divorce.
4. You use up 150 calories every time you make love.
5. The marriage age in India is the lowest in the world, with 20 years for males and 14.5 years for females. At the other end of the extreme is Ireland, with 31.4 years for males and 26.5 years for females.
6. If you're looking for a husband, don't go to the USSR. According to a recent census it has the largest recorded shortage of males to go around, a mere 1,000 for every 1,145.9 females.
7. Marriage is on the upswing. For the seventh year in a row, the number of newly marrieds is hovering around 2.5 million.
8. The divorce rate is dropping. Within the last year it declined about 4 percent from 5.3 per 1,000 people to 5.1 per 1,000 people.
9. Marriage makes people happy. In a recent survey, over 100,000 people were asked to rate various aspects of their lives in terms of happiness. Married women ranked marriage #2 on a ten-point scale, and married men rated it #3.

10. Jack V. and Edna Moran of Seattle, Washington, love each other so much they've become the most married couple, claiming a world's record of 40 ceremonies since the first and only necessary occasion took place in Seaside, Oregon, on July 27, 1937.

ABOUT THE AUTHORS

MARCIA ROSEN is a freelance writer and co-owner of Northern News Service International, a Connecticut-based news agency serving magazines and newspapers throughout the United States and Europe. She lives in Stamford, Connecticut with her husband and two children.

JOANNA MAGDA POLENZ, M.D., is the senior attending psychiatrist at Phelps Memorial Hospital and a member of the American Board of Psychiatry and Neurology in Psychiatry. She is the author of *In Defense of Marriage* (Gardner Press, New York, 1981). Dr. Polenz, her husband and three children live in Briarcliff Manor, New York.